T0090354

Nipissing

From
Brulé
To
Booth

By
Murray Leatherdale

Second Edition

2nd Edition
Editor: T. A. Grainger
Visual Design Coordinator: T. A. Grainger

Order this book online at www.trafford.com
or email orders@trafford.com

Most Trafford titles are also available at major online book retailers.

Print information available on the last page.

ISBN: 978-1-4251-5342-7 (sc)
ISBN: 978-1-4251-5343-4 (e)

Trafford rev. 06/21/2019

 www.trafford.com

North America & international
toll-free: 1 888 232 4444 (USA & Canada)
fax: 812 355 4082

The author dedicated the first edition of this book to, "... the Memory of my father, *GORDON LEATHERDALE* whose keen interest in Canadiana inspired the research for this book."

The second edition of this book is dedicated to the author, *DR. MURRAY LEATHERDALE (1927-1984)* by his wife and children.

The republishing of this book testifies to our heightened appreciation of the heritage he imparted to us, and is a legacy not only for his grandchildren with whom he was allowed so little time, but also for the City of North Bay that he so dearly loved.

He is forever in our hearts.

Holly, Trudy, Libby, Myles and Lauran

What started as a simple summer project turned into several years of frustration and discovery that would not have been realized without the help and guidance of many people. From ownership to structure to simple words of encouragement, the Family wishes to thank all who contributed to the completion of this project, with special recognition to the following:

Ralph Celentano
Adam Gour
John D'Agostino
John Kooistra
Ione Barré

Thank You

This well-worn, first-run (1975) copy of Murray's book (shown here in black & white) belongs to his daughter, Libby. Its tattered state bears witness to the many readings it has endured over the years and its value as a source of entertainment and reference.

ABOUT THE AUTHOR

Born May 25, 1927 in Orillia, Ontario, William Murray Leatherdale was the first of three sons born to Gordon and Maurine (nee Taylor). His romance with Canadiana began at an early age. Tutored by his father in the ways of the wilderness, he hunted and fished throughout Huronia. His passion for the outdoors, and his interest in the history and people of these lands, led him to become an avid sportsman, conservationist and researcher. His ability to pilot a plane, guide a canoe, drive a dog team, and survive the most northern of woods, allowed him to witness the solace and beauty of our lakes and forests. He developed a keen "bush sense" and often searched for signs of early inhabitants, native encampments and routes of our early explorers while enjoying our natural environment.

The year 1953 was an especially important one for Murray. He received his chiropractic degree, married Holly Antler and moved with her to North Bay, Ontario to set up practice. With a desire to relieve suffering and promote wellness, Murray offered free clinics to crippled children, extending his practice to Thorne and Mattawa, in Ontario, and to Temiscaming in Quebec. He also founded the Northern Ontario Chiropractic Association, and sat on the board as president during these early years.

The City of North Bay was the beneficiary of Murray's deep sense of civic duty and seemingly boundless energies. He recognized the ecological wonders of the area and, although he had no desire to change or re-make the city, he endeavoured to make it more prosperous, and a "must visit" place on the map. To this end, in the 1960's and '70's he sat as president for the Chamber of Commerce, the North Bay Historical Society, and the Hunters and Anglers Association. It was within the latter organization that he lobbied Queen's Park to pass the "Safe Gun Handling" course into law. In 1977 he promoted the formation of the North Bay Area Museum (now Discovery North Bay), served as chairman, and was later awarded a lifetime membership. Murray was proclaimed North Bay's "Citizen of the Year" in 1975 and he was awarded the 'Dorothy Walford Memorial Award' from the North Bay–Mattawa Conservation Authority in 1980, an organization which he had served as a board member. Murray had the opportunity to combine his love of nature and sporting activities with his historical research when, in 1966, he helped establish the "Ville Marie to North Bay Canoe Race," reviving the old Voyageur routes. He further brought attention to the indigenous peoples and early explorers by restoring and maintaining some of their routes through the area, primarily the La Vase Portages and the raising and placing of historical monuments and plaques in strategic locations, noting the importance of these passages. As his research progressed he became convinced that a fort had existed at the mouth of the La Vase River, and so he founded the "Restoration of Fort Laronde Society." He encouraged archaeological verification of this site, as well as

The Author, Dr. Murray Leatherdale – 1954

others located on Trout Lake. To authenticate his research, digs have been undertaken at the mouth of the La Vase River, in what is now Champlain Park.

In the late 1960's, Murray's sporting activities branched into dog sled racing. At one point he could claim ownership of 60 sled dogs, including Alaskan, Siberian and even Greyhound mixes. He co-founded the award-winning North Bay Winter Fur Carnival, of which the Towers International Sled Dog Derby was a part. He further brought notoriety to his community by taking the late Pierre Elliot Trudeau on a dog sled ride while the then Prime Minister was on a visit to North Bay. Murray and a group of fellow "mushers" brought international attention to this community when a Guinness World Record was attained with the formation of a hitched sled team of fifty dogs!

Most would say, however, that Murray was at his best when enlightening others about our historical past through his many lectures and stories. His rare gift for making the past come alive made him a noted lecturer throughout Ontario. His passionate rhetoric, vision of bygone eras, and dedication to his community culminated in the publishing of Nipissing from Brulé to Booth in 1975. He presented the original manuscript in honour of the city's 50th Anniversary. Sponsored by and dedicated to the North Bay and District Chamber of Commerce, it was meant as a fund raising project, and indeed it was, as the volume had three printings.

While focusing on finding the actual site of Fort Laronde and researching and planning for his second book, Murray suffered a massive stroke. December 1, 1978, brought an end to the diverse and enriched career of William Murray Leatherdale, Doctor of Chiropractic, sportsman, pilot, storyteller and author. But, however diminished, the man remained. With the right side of his body paralysed and communication severely diminished, Murray's need to express the storyteller within led him to take up painting, perhaps providing a connection with others that he could no longer achieve through conversation. Murray painted and traveled until his death on June 11, 1984.

Murray's passage through this life, although short, was lived to its fullest, and should the Algonquin legend of the "happy hunting grounds," which he writes of in this book, be true, his journey continues – perhaps sitting on the porch of Eustache Laronde's cabin at the mouth of the La Vase exchanging tales of past adventures, and in the quiet moments listening to the steady stroke of the Voyageurs' paddles as the great Montreal canoes, laden over the gunwales with supplies, continue their journey west. Or, whole again, he could just as easily be relishing in the struggle with a pack of furs, weighing more than himself, over a portage on the way to Montreal with his fellow Voyageurs. Surely, his historical knowledge will provide him an eternity of people to meet, experiences to enjoy and stories to tell.

This book is one of two projects of the North Bay and District Chamber of Commerce commemorating the 50th anniversary of the City of North Bay in 1975. The other Chamber project [being] the North Bay Dollar . . . described on page 12 [in the 1st edition].

'Nipissing from Brulé to Booth' reflects on the early Indian society and arrival of the district's first white men, the voyageurs, explorers and missionaries. We hope that it will stimulate and encourage its readers to pursue the study of the fascinating history of Canada's past.

We are indebted to the author, Dr. Murray Leatherdale, for the countless hours of research and writing he spent on behalf of the Chamber preparing this book. We also gratefully acknowledge the efforts of Bert Saunders who prepared all the artwork [first edition].

Any profit realized from this publication [first edition] will be channelled back into the community by way of the many civic projects of this Chamber of Commerce.

BOARD OF DIRECTORS – 1975

Art Braund	Geoffrey Matthews
Gordon F. Brown	Stan May, (President)
M. J. Colyer	Daphne J. Mayne, (2nd Vice Pres.)
Gary Corbett	James McGinn, (1st Vice President)
Don Crozier (Treasurer)	Ed Morandin
Glen DeVuono (Manager)	Terrence O'Connell
Bud Gennoe	J. K. Picken
Wayne Glass	Frank Schaffer
Maurice Guevremont	Gerd Schutz
Harry Hall	John Sinden
Al Hart	Hartley Trussler
John J. Lyle, (Past Pres.)	Ed Vitunski

Original Illustrations by Bert Saunders

ÉTIENNE BRÛLÉ

Additional Illustrations by *T. A. Grainger.*

TABLE of CONTENTS

INTRODUCTION, first edition

by Murray Leatherdale

For the past two decades [1955-1975], I have been fascinated with the important historical role Lake Nipissing, the Mattawa and French Rivers played in Canadian history.

During this time I have been involved in extensive research of our area, and discovered that this route had immense significance to the local Indians, to the explorers, and to the fur traders and lumbermen.

Thus when the North Bay & District Chamber of Commerce suggested I write a short brochure for local and tourist interest, I suggested that I had sufficient notes to write a more lengthy account of our early history.

The Chamber accepted this proposal and the result is this study.

The intention, then, is to provide a survey of the early years in the Nipissing area, in the years before the white settlement began in earnest. The later period is the subject of a study currently being prepared by Mr. Hartley Trussler. Also in 1961 the late William Kennedy published his book, North Bay, which deals with the early history of the city of North Bay.

In this book I have attempted to focus the applicable Canadian history onto the Nipissing area; consequently it was necessary to make several geographical wanderings. It was not my intention to re-write Canadian history, but only to direct attention to that part which applied to this area.

I had hoped to deal with the Nipissing Indians on a more personal basis, by following the chiefs by name, and by tracing families and groups through several generations or even centuries. This turned out to be impossible. The chief source of data for this very early period is the writing of the Jesuits, and in very few cases do these refer to the Nipissings by their individual or family names. This was a disappointment, but I am pleased that my research was able to reveal the general story of the Nipissing tribe, from the time of their first contacts with Europeans to the present.

The research for this book was done almost entirely from the original source material in The Jesuit Relations and the personal diaries of various explorers. The Jesuit Relations for those not familiar with them is a collection of letters and reports sent home to the Father

Provincial in France by the Jesuit Missionaries in New France. They span the period from 1605 to 1795, and deal with a geographical area from the Bay of Fundy to Lake Superior and from the St. Lawrence basin to the mouth of the Mississippi. For the most part they deal with Huronia and Quebec. They have been translated and collected into an English edition by Reuben Thwaites, and this collection fills 73 volumes.

I would like to thank a number of people who assisted me in collecting data and writing this book. Charles Laberge, Deputy of the Samuel Champlain Park in Mattawa, Gordon Restoule of Dokis Bay and the French River, Doris Kennedy of North Bay, Patricia Wilkinson of Corbeil, Mrs. Donald McIntosh of Powassan and Miss Clarkson and the staff of the North Bay Public Library all assisted me in providing research materials. Donald Sawyer, a native Ojibway from North Bay, introduced me to various Ontario Indians and provided me with insight into the Ojibway culture and language. His assistance was most helpful. And thanks to Lawrence Commanda, a Nipissing Indian, who introduced me to local legends. I also want to thank William MacBrien of Mattawa who provided the solitude of his Blue Lake fishing camp at which the greater portion of the book was written, and Robert J. Surtees who assisted in the editing. Glen DeVuono and his secretarial staff at the Chamber of Commerce of Shirley Larson, Shelley Brown and Leigh Beckler assisted greatly by photocopying documents and by typing the manuscript. And of course my wife, Holly, who helped me not only by typing the original draft but also by providing constant encouragement, must receive very special thanks.

tag

Part One
The Nipissing Indians

Chapter 1

The Nipissing Passageway and Its Glacial History

In this study I have attempted to focus Canadian history onto an area that stretches from the confluence of the Mattawa and Ottawa Rivers, up the Mattawa River to Trout Lake, over the La Vase portages (the height of land), across Lake Nipissing and down the French River to its mouth at Georgian Bay. This route played an important part in the discovery of Canada, and as a route of transportation for its riches. It was used continuously during the seventeenth, eighteenth and nineteenth centuries by explorers, fur traders, missionaries and lumbermen. Part of it is used today as the course for the annual Ville Marie to North Bay canoe race and is considered by many as one of the finest recreation areas in Ontario. North Bay straddles the height of land between Lake Nipissing, drained by the French River as it cuts its way through the Precambrian Shield, and Trout Lake, drained by the Mattawa River, which cuts through the Shield in the opposite direction. Both of these rivers eventually work their way into the same St. Lawrence River system. But this whole water system is, in geological terms, a relatively current event.

During the Precambrian era, several million years ago, violent upheavals occurred in the earth's crust. Volcanic eruption and earthquakes produced folding and faulting, creating massive rock surfaces which have become known as the Precambrian or Laurentian Shield, and which covers almost two thirds of Canada. Following the Precambrian era the valley of the Nipissing passage was submerged beneath raging seas. The sand, clay and lime deposits formed into limestone, shale and sandstone. The basic character of the Nipissing passageway was thus shaped millions of years before the first ice age. During the waning of the Wisconsin ice age, the last of the four glacial ages, the Great Lakes evolved through several stages. At one point about 11,000 years ago, when the Nipissing passage was buried under an enormous weight of ice, perhaps two miles thick, the Great Lakes drained through the Champlain sea. This was a vast body of water formed by the Atlantic Ocean flooding up the St. Lawrence and Ottawa Valleys as far as the present town of Deep River on the Ottawa. About 10,000 years ago the glacier had retreated far enough to uncover the Nipissing passage. Although Lakes Ontario and Erie still drained into the receding Champlain Sea, Lakes Stanley and Hough, two lakes then occupying the approximate area that Lake Huron now fills, emptied directly into Lake Nipissing and then down the Mattawa and Ottawa Rivers to the Champlain Sea. The present site of North Bay was then the floor of a raging river. At its lowest the Mattawa discharge may have been as low as sea level. The evidence that this discharge was a long, major river may be seen in various pot or pit formations along the French River. The most spectacular of these, however, are probably at Talon Chutes on the Mattawa just below Lake Talon. The latter are circular kettle-like erosions in the softer limestone type rocks, two of them large enough to hold three adults, and deep enough to come to shoulder level. They are located on a rocky prominence about sixty feet above the river surface. They were formed by the swirling of harder rocks in the turbulent water, creating erosion throughout the years.

At this time about 10,000 years ago, there probably were primitive peoples wandering along the shores of Lake Nipissing. These aborigines were known as Paleo-Indians. They lived by hunting game with primitive stone weapons and gathering berries and roots. They had not learned to use the canoe as their Algonkian descendants would so skilfully use. But they did rely on stone, mainly for the building of their abodes. Occasionally relics of their past are unearthed throughout the province.

As the glacier continued to retreat, the land in the north, relieved of the great weight of ice pressing down upon it, started to rise. As the Mattawa discharge (also known as the North Bay outlet) rose, drainage of the Great Lakes occurred at a slower rate. This in turn initiated the Nipissing stage of the Great Lakes, about 6,000 years ago, which was characterized by a vastly larger Lake Huron. For a time drainage of the upper Great Lakes continued by three routes, mainly the Nipissing and Mattawa, by the lower Great Lakes and St. Lawrence, and from the Michigan basin into the Mississippi River.

The ongoing uplift of land, however, closed off the Mattawa valley as an outlet for the Great Lakes, perhaps 4200 years ago, and created a height of land between the drainage systems of Lake Huron and the Ottawa River. Today Lake Nipissing drains westward by way of the French River into Lake Huron, and the Mattawa River no longer has its source in Lake Nipissing.

The corridor from Lake Nipissing to the confluence of the Mattawa and Ottawa Rivers, at one time as low as the level of the sea, today registers 640 feet above sea level at Lake Nipissing, 663 feet at Trout Lake and 485 feet at the mouth of the Mattawa.

Chapter 2
The Nipissing Indians

The Nipissing Indians were known to the early French explorers and missionaries as Bissiriniens, Nepissirians, Nepissings, Nipissiriniens, Nipistingues, and to their Huron allies as Askik-wanehronans. All of these names translate to mean "people of the little water," a reference to their main location on Lake Nipissing, a lake of small dimensions in comparison to the Lake of the Hurons. The precise details of their arrival in this area are unknown. It appears, however, that long before the arrival of the Europeans, a large tribe of Ojibway around what is now Sault Ste. Marie divided into three groups: the Potawatomi who spread south through the Michigan peninsula; the Ottawas who located across the northern shore of the Georgian Bay and the Manitoulin Island; and the Nipissings who settled in the area of Lake Nipissing and the Upper French River.

The Nipissings then are a branch of the Ojibway Tribal organization, which, in turn, is part of the Algonquin linguistic group, which dominated in the eastern woodlands of North America. Because all tribes of the Algonquin were basically nomadic, it is difficult to assign a specific location to any of them. Certain tribes, or bands, did tend to occupy certain areas, however, and thus we can say that the Nipissings tended to base themselves around the lake that bears their name.

Most of their villages were found around Lake Nipissing itself, mainly on the north shore, but there were some also on the upper French River and a few on Trout Lake. Their hunting grounds extended north to Lake Temagami, east to the Ottawa River and Lake Temiskaming, west along the French River to its mouth, south into Algonquin Park and the northern half of the District of Parry Sound. They lived by the chase, and ignored agriculture. The family hunting ground formed the basis of their socio-economic organization, and intruders into the family hunting area were liable to be put to death. This was apparently not an idle possibility, for the neighbouring tribes were said to have feared the Nipissings as "sorcerers." The Nipissings were also traders, and even in pre-European days they had commercial dealings with their neighbours.

South of them, on the Ottawa River, was a tribe of Algonquins, with headquarters, according to Champlain, at Allumette Island near modern Pembroke. It was from this island, named by the French, that they took their name. West of the Nipissings, from the mouth of the French River to the Manitoulin Island, lived the Ottawas, known to Champlain as the "Cheveaux Releves" (the High Hairs). In the area between Lake Simcoe and Georgian Bay, north as far as the Severn River, were the Hurons. South of this area, between what is now Collingwood and Owen Sound, were the Tobaccos (or Petuns), and in the Niagara Fruitland and escarpment lived the Neutrals. These last three tribes spoke the Iroquoian tongue, which was the other major language of the eastern woodlands.

The Nipissings had contacts with all these tribes, and many more to the north and west. The trade of the area expanded after the arrival of the French, because of the greater variety of marketable goods, but even before this the Nipissings had conducted trade in all directions, dealing in corn, fish, tobacco, furs and later the French trade goods. Although they did produce some of these items themselves, notably the pickerel from Lake Nipissing, the Nipissings held largely a middleman position in this commerce. In this respect they were similar to the Hurons. They would travel as far west as Sault Ste. Marie and Lake Superior, and as far north as James Bay. The latter journey, which Champlain once planned to take, required forty days. The Jesuits on several occasions described the Nipissings' disappearance up the river La Fountaine (the Sturgeon River); and little imagination would be required to picture them travelling as well on Lake Temagami, Anima Nipissing, the Montreal River, Watabig Lake, the Frederick House River, and the Abitibi Route.

Furs from this northern region were taken ultimately to Tadoussac, on the north shore of the St. Lawrence at the mouth of the Saguenay. This location had been a North American market place long before the coming of the white man, and here, items, including sea shells from as far away as Florida, would be traded for prime beaver from as great a distance as Hudson's Bay. Champlain accidentally bisected this trade route when he settled on the St. Lawrence, and the Indians were very quick to see the advantage of trading for European goods in preference to seashells.

It was the annual custom of the Nipissings to leave in the autumn with great catches of fish (apparently the delicacy and fame of the Nipissing pickerel was known many centuries before the white man invented the tourist industry) to spend the winter with their Huron neighbours, exchanging fish for corn. Father Gabriel Lalemant described this event in the Relation of 1640.

Father Gabriel Lalemant
Spent a great deal of time among the Nipissings until his torture and death at the hands of the Iroquois along side Father Jean de Brebeuf.

The Askikwanehronons, according to our Hurons — or Nipissiriniens, according to the Algonquins — form a Nation of the Algonquin tongue which contains more wandering than settled people. They seem to have as many abodes as the year has seasons; in the Spring a part of them remain for fishing, where they consider it the best, a part go away to trade with the tribes which gather on the shore of the North or icy sea, upon which they voyage ten days, after having spent thirty days upon the rivers, in order to reach it.

In summer, they all gather together, on the road of the Hurons to the French, on the border of a large lake which bears their name, and is about two hundred leagues distant from Quebec, and about seventy from our Hurons; so that their principal dwelling place is, as it were, two-thirds of the way from Quebec to the country of our Hurons.

About the middle of autumn, they begin to approach our Hurons, upon whose lands they generally spend the winter; but, before reaching them, they catch as many fish as possible, which they dry. This is the ordinary money with which they buy their main stock of corn, although they come supplied with all other goods, as they are a rich people and live in comfort. They cultivate a little land near their summer dwelling; but it is more for pleasure, and that they may have fresh food to eat, than for their support.

Our fathers at Quebec, and at the Three Rivers, who in the past have successfully laboured for the improvement of all the wandering tribes which were nearest to them, and have made nearly all of them men and Christians, cast their eyes upon this Nation, the nearest to the last one which came down in order to settle near them. But as these no longer came for Trade, on account of some opposition that others from below made against them, they did not know how to broach this matter.

Last summer God was pleased so to order things that they themselves resolved to feel their way, and to send some canoes for the Trade with the French. They arrived safely, without any difficulty, and nothing would have happened more opportunely for that which we desired.

Consequently we spoke to them, not of abandoning their country and coming to place themselves near the other Algonquins already settled, but rather of receiving a few of our Fathers among them, that they might be instructed; they declared that this would be very acceptable to them. This is why Fathers Claude Pijart, and Charles

Raymbault, setting out from below to come and help us, had directions to offer themselves, on the way, to them. But not having found them at their summer dwelling, and having learned that they were to come and winter in our quarters, they landed here without losing hope of seeing those to whom they were specially sent.

They were not disappointed in their expectation. These Savages, numbering about two hundred and fifty souls, arrived shortly after, and took such a district in this country, for their winter quarters, that it seems to have been the Holy Ghost, and no other, who guided them.

They chose their ground on the same side of the river, upon which we were, and at two arquebus shots from our house. It was precisely from not being inconvenienced by their nearness to us, and also from our not being very distant from them, that our Fathers were easily able, every day, to go and instruct them; which they did not fail to do.

We must admit that Tribes like these have as indescribably greater aptitude of heart for the seed of Faith than have our Hurons. The Fathers had not talked with them for a fortnight, before they took the utmost delight in listening to them; and they had no greater satisfaction than when they were taught to chant the greatness of God, the articles of belief, and the Commandments. In a word, nothing most pleasing can be found than the way and manner in which, from the first, they bore themselves toward the Fathers.

In the beginning the chief Captain of this Tribe, named Wikasoumir, made a public announcement that every one should pray to God and honour him, in the way taught by the French.

After that, the little children began to learn the first principles of the Faith, and applied themselves so that in a short time they were found remarkably advanced therein.

They make no difficulty about permitting their sick to be instructed and baptized; some of them even contribute willingly to their own instruction. A few have been baptized in that condition, to whom it pleased God to restore health.

Nevertheless the Fathers have not yet been able to decide upon baptizing any one who is in health, although they have been urgently entreated to do so, as they desire to make a longer proof of their firmness and constancy; and, in order to do this, they resolved to follow them to the place where these are going for the rest of the year, and by this very means to advance and become still more and more proficient in the use of their language, which in many respects *appears to be different with the Algonquins in the districts below. They set out from here, all together, on the eighth of May, the day before the Ascension, with the hope of arriving at the principal dwelling place of this Tribe by Whitsunday. May it please that adorable Spirit whose name their mission bears, to take perfect possession both of the minds and hearts of those poor Tribes, and of our own, and to reign therein eternally.*

The opportunity we had of instructing the Nipissiriniens, on account of their nearness, and the great aptitude they showed in receiving instruction during the short time that their wintering lasted, made us unable to abandon them and devote ourselves to others of the same language, who had also come to winter in the country. However, Father Claude Pijart visited a few other places, in one of which he found perhaps five hundred persons gathered together of different tribes, to whom, in passing, he spoke of the Kingdom of God, and caused them to sing God's praises. Nearly everywhere he found some predestined soul, which was only awaiting his visit that it might ascend to Heaven. I will note a rather remarkable instance of this.

The Tontthrataronons, an Algonquin tribe, numbering about fifteen cabins, were wintering upon the lands of the Mission of Saint Jean Baptiste to the Arendaehronons. Father Claude Pijart, on going to visit them, received from them every manner of hearty welcome. When the evening came, as he was almost asleep, he heard a plaintive voice, he asked what it was, they told him that it was a poor sick old woman, who was in the next cabin, and who was dying. The father begged to go and see her; the head of the Cabin, an important Captain, arose and lighted a torch, that is to say, a piece of bark; and, the Father being at a loss for water for the baptism, this Captain quickly melted some snow for him. The Father entered, instructed this poor creature, and questioned her; she gave him full satisfaction, as if she had been long instructed; he baptized her, and shortly after she died happily.

The Father found in all those whom he visited, a disposition of mind similar to that which he found in the Nipissiriniens: but it was much better in those who travelled most, and had most frequented the warehouse of our Frenchmen at the Three Rivers and at Quebec for some years past. We shall see that with time, and with the reinforcement that we are hoping for in this language, we shall be able to do more, in the future, for all these poor wandering sheep, as well of the one language as the other.

The Nipissings had been in the habit of wintering with the Hurons long before the coming of the whites and Champlain paid their winter village a visit in 1615. Why the Jesuits passing through Lake Nipissing regularly and this tribe wintering in Huronia annually had been overlooked by these missionaries until 1640 is a mystery to me. Perhaps the good Fathers had their hands full Christianizing the elusive Hurons and ducking the Iroquois.

At any rate we have now established that in 1640 the Nipissings had their very own mission, "The Holy Ghost" or "Mission d'Esprit." Incidentally, to follow the Jesuit Relations, consider one league to be three miles.

The Indians, like our modern sportsmen, found the spring fishing on Nipissing to be the best. We discover that two Jesuits have been placed in charge of the Nipissing mission, Father Claude Pijart and Charles Raymbault.

The Relations tell us that in Huronia were found 250 Nipissing souls. But, I have discovered in my research that wild guesses were made as to the number of Indians in any given spot. Champlain claims 7,000 met him at Lake Nipissing. Other Jesuits claim that the entire coast of Lake Nipissing was completely covered by dwellings (which of course is exaggerated).

I feel that if Pijart and Raymbault found only 250 that winter, all the Nipissings did not go to Huronia, or others had wandered off to other Huron villages. Choosing to camp on the same side of the river, I gather to be in the vicinity of the main Huron mission, Ste. Marie, on the Wye River near Midland.

Two years later, in 1642, Pijart founded a second mission for the Nipissings, St. Elizabeth. The location of this mission was probably near the shore of Lake Couchiching, half a mile south of Washago, just after crossing the Trent waterway. Probably Highway 11 passes right through the site.

The mission was used until the invasion and massacre of the Hurons by the Iroquois in 1648.

The Algonquins from the Ottawa River also wintered here and shared in the use of St. Elizabeth as well as their own mission of St. Jean Baptiste near Hawkestone on Lake Simcoe.

These tribes wintered mainly with the Hurons in fear of Iroquois attacks. The Iroquois were as formidable a foe on snowshoes as by canoe.

After break-up in the spring of 1641, Fathers Claude Pijart and Charles Raymbault returned with the Nipissing to Lake Nipissing to carry on the mission of the Holy Ghost. The Nipissings are mentioned prominently in the relations of 1642 also. In that report Father Lalemant describes in great detail the Nipissing Feast of the Dead. It is the most complete available description of that phase of the Nipissings' way of life.

> *In this country, and with the Nations who do not differ from us more in Climate and in Language than they do in their nature, their way of acting, and their opinions, and in everything that can exist in Man, except body and soul, it takes time to realize the situation. Still more is needed to introduce among them the knowledge and ideas of a GOD whose name had never been mentioned here: of a law that has never been received here; of a manner of life wholly different from that which has been led here for two, three, even four thousand years. Now, the experience of the past has enlightened us considerably as to the means that must be adopted for the Conversion of the Hurons; but it must be confessed that we are still very much in the dark as regards the Algonquins who dwell in these Countries that are more remote from the Fort of our French people.*

> *They lead the nomad life of people scattered here and there, wherever the chase or the fishing may lead them, sometimes in the woods, sometimes over rocks, or on islands in the middle of some great lake; sometimes on the banks of rivers, without a roof, without a house or fixed residence; without gathering anything from the earth, beyond what it yields in a barren Country to those who have never cultivated it. It is necessary to follow these Peoples, if we wish to Christianize them; but, as they continually divide themselves up, we cannot devote ourselves to some without wandering from the others.*

> *Last year, we had here only two of our Fathers who spoke the Algonquin language, Father Claude Pijart and Father Charles Raymbault. God's Providence brought to them at our doors, during the winter, the Nipissiriniens whom they had commenced to instruct. When these peoples left us after the Ice had melted, the same fathers followed them.*

> *If in this wandering life there be greater danger on the water than on land; if sufferings must be borne in these shifting Houses; if,*

during the heat of Summer, fatigue must be endured in making journeys whereon can be found no shelter, no provisions, nor furniture, other than the little that one carries with him, and whereon one is even obliged in going across the land to transport on his shoulders the Canoe that has borne him over the water; if anything still more arduous than all that, is trying to one's nature, Heaven does not fail us in these necessities; and we find by experience that it is not always true that the fatigued body weighs down the Soul. In any case the two Fathers remained there all summer, continuing to instruct those poor Peoples. But to make a Christian out of a Barbarian is not the work of a day. The seed that is sown one year in the earth does not bear fruit so soon. A great step is gained when one has learned to know those with whom he has to deal; has penetrated their thoughts; has adapted himself to their language, their customs, and their manner of living; and, when necessary, has been a Barbarian with them, in order to win them over to Jesus Christ.

This has been no slight influence in soothing these People, and in removing from their minds the bad impressions that had been given them of the truths of our Faith, that God has so blessed the labours of our Fathers that, out of many children who were dangerously ill and who were baptized, all recovered their health. Therefore it was that the parents, who witnessed this blessing of Heaven conferred on these little Christians, procured this happiness for them as soon as possible, when they saw them in danger.

Toward the end of the summer, these Peoples turned their thoughts to the celebration of their feast of the dead, which is to collect the bones of their deceased relatives, and, by way of honour to their memory, to procure for them a more honourable sepulchre than that which had enclosed them since their death. This solemnity, among the Nomad Tribes up here, is accompanied by rites of some importance, differing much from those of our Hurons, which may be seen in previous Relations; and it may perhaps be interesting to learn some further particulars about them, which I shall set down here.

The day was appointed, at the beginning of September, for all the confederated Nations, who were invited thereto by Envoys expressly sent. The spot selected for the purpose was at a Bay of the great Lake, distant about twenty leagues from the country of the Hurons. Having been invited to attend, I thought that I ought to take advantage of the opportunity that GOD gave me to establish closer relations with these Barbarians, so as to secure, in the future, better means for the advancement of his Glory among them. The number of persons present was about two thousand.

Those of each Nation, before landing, in order to make their entry more imposing, form their Canoes in line, and wait until others come to meet them. When the People are assembled, the Chief stands up in the middle of his Canoe, and states the object that has brought him hither. Thereupon each one throws away some portion of his goods to be scrambled for. Some articles float on the water, while others sink to the bottom. The young men hasten to the spot. One will seize a mat, wrought as tapestries are in France; another a Beaver skin; others get a hatchet, or a dish, or some Porcelain beads, or other article, each according to his skill and the good fortune he may have. There is nothing but joy, cries, and public acclamations, to which the Rocks surrounding the great Lake return an Echo that drowns all their voices.

When the Nations are assembled, and divided, each in their own seats, Beaver Robes, skins of Otter, of Caribou, of wild Cats, and of Moose; Hatchets, Kettles, Porcelain Beads, and all things that are precious in this Country, are exhibited. Each Chief of a Nation presents his own gift to those who hold the feast, giving to each present some name that seems best suited to it. As for us, the presents that we gave were not for the purpose of drying their tears, or consoling them for the death of the deceased; but that we might wish to the living the same happiness that we hope to enjoy in Heaven when they shall have acknowledged the same GOD whom we serve on Earth. This kind of present astonished them at first, as not being according to their usage. But we gave them to understand that only the hope that we had of seeing them become Christians led us to desire their friendship.

After that, it was a pleasure characterized by nothing of savagery, to witness in the midst of this Barbarism a Ballet danced by forty persons, to the sound of voices and of a sort of drum, in such harmonious accord that they rendered all the tones that are most agreeable in Music.

The dance consisted of three parts. The first represented various encounters of enemies in single combat, one pursuing his foe, hatchet in hand, to give him the deathblow, while at the same time he seems to receive it himself, by losing his advantage; he regains it, and after a great many feints, all performed in time with the music, he finally overcomes his antagonist, and returns victorious. Another, with different movements, fences, javelin in hand; this one is armed with arrows; his enemy provides himself with a buckler that covers him, and strikes a blow at him with a club. They are three different personages, not one of whom is armed like the others; their gestures, their movements, their steps, their glances, in a word, everything that can be seen, is different in each one; and yet in so complete accord with one another that it seems as if but one mind governed these irregular movements.

Hardly was this combat ended than the Musicians arose; and we witnessed, as the Second Part, a dance on a large scale, first by eight persons, then by twelve, then by sixteen, ever increasing in proportion, who quickened or checked their steps according to the voices that gave the measure.

The Women then suddenly appeared, and danced the Third Part of this Ball, which was as agreeable as the others, and in no wise offensive to modesty. The inhabitants of the Sault, who came to this feast from a distance of a hundred or a hundred and twenty leagues, were Actors in this Ballet.

A Pole of considerable height had been set in the ground. A Nipissirinien climbed to the top of it, and tied there two prizes, a Kettle, and the skin of a Deer, and called upon the young men to display their agility. Although the bark had been stripped from the Pole, and it was quite smooth, he greased it, to make it more difficult to grasp. No sooner had he descended, than several pressed forward to climb it. Some lost courage at the beginning, others at a greater or lesser height; and one, who almost reached the top, suddenly found himself at the bottom. No one could attain the top; but there was a Huron who provided himself with a knife and some cord, and, after having made reasonable efforts until he reached the middle of the Pole, he had recourse to cunning. He drew his knife, and cut notches in the tree, in which he placed his cord; then making a stirrup of it, he supported and raised himself higher, and continued to do so until he attained the prizes suspended there in spite of the hooting and shouting of the Audience. Having grasped these, he slid to the ground, and reembarked to go to Kebac, whither his journey led him.

This unfair conduct led the Algonquin Captains to make a Public complaint, which was deemed reasonable; and the Hurons taxed themselves for a present of Porcelain Beads to repair this injustice, which caused the Souls of the deceased to weep.

After this, the election of the Nipissirinien Chiefs took place. When the votes were taken, the chief Captain arose, and called them each by name. They made their appearance, clothed in their finest robes.

When they had received their Commissions, they gave largess of a quantity of Beaver skins and Moose hides, in order to make themselves known, and that they might be received with applause in their Offices.

This Election was followed by the Resurrection of those Persons of importance who had died since the last Feast; which means that, in accordance with the custom of the Country, their names were transferred to some of their relatives, so as to perpetuate their memory.

On the following day, the Women were occupied in fitting up, in a superb manner, a Cabin with an arched roof, about a hundred paces long, the width and height of which were in proportion.

Although the Riches of this Country are not sought for in the bowels of the Earth, and although most of them consist only in the spoils of Animals, nevertheless, if they were transported to Europe, they would have their value. The presents that the Nipissiriniens gave to the other Nations alone would have cost in France forty or even fifty thousand francs.

After that, the same Women carried the bones of the Dead into this magnificent Room. These bones were enclosed in caskets of bark, covered with new robes of Beaver skins, and enriched with collars and scarfs of Porcelain Beads.

Near each Dead body sat the women, in two lines, facing each other. Then entered the Captains, who acted as Stewards and carried the dishes containing food. This feast is for the Women only, because they evince a deeper feeling of mourning.

Afterward, about a dozen Men with carefully selected voices entered the middle of the Cabin, and began to sing a most lugubrious chant, which, being seconded by the Women in the refrains, was very sweet and sad.

The gloom of the night conduced not a little to this Mourning; and the darkness, lighted only by the flickering flames of two fires which had been kindled at each end of the Cabin, received their wailings and their sighs. The theme of the song consisted in a sort of homage paid to the Demon whom they involved, and to whom their lamentations were addressed. This chant continued through the night, amid deep silence on the part of the Audience, who seemed to have only respect and admiration for so sacred a ceremony.

On the following morning, these Women distributed corn, moccasins, and other small articles that are within their means, or the products of their industry. Their chant ever plaintive, and interspersed with sobs, seemed to be addressed to the Souls of the deceased, whom they sped on their way as it appeared, with deep regret by continually waving branches that they held in their hands, for fear that these poor souls might be surprised by the dread of war and the terror of arms, and that their rest might thus be disturbed. For, at the same time, the body of an Army could be observed descending a neighbouring Mountain with frightful cries and yells, running around at first in a circle, then in an oval; and, at last, after a thousand other figures they rushed upon the Cabin, of which they became Masters, the Women having yielded the place, as if to an Enemy.

These Warriors became Dancers after this Victory. Each Nation, in turn, occupied the Ballroom, for the purpose of displaying their agility, until the Algonquin Captains, who acted as masters of Ceremonies, entered ten or twelve in line, bearing flour, beavers, and some dogs still alive, with which they prepared a splendid Feast for the Hurons. The Algonquin Nations were served apart, as their Language is entirely different from the Huron.

Afterward, two Meetings were held; one consisted of the Algonquins who had been invited to this Solemnity, to whom various presents were given, according to the extent of the Alliance that existed between the Nipissiriniens and them. The bones of the Dead were borne between the presents given to the most intimate friends, and were accompanied by the most precious robes and by collars of porcelain beads, which are the gold, the pearls, and the diamonds of this Country.

The second Assembly was that of the Huron Nations, at which the Nipissiriniens gave us the highest seat, the first titles of honour, and marks of affection above all their Confederates. Here new presents were given, and so lavishly that not a single Captain withdrew empty-handed.

The Feast concluded with prizes given for physical strength, for bodily skill, and for agility. Even the Women took part in this contest, and everything was done with such moderation and reserve that at least, in watching them, one would never have thought that he was in the midst of an assemblage of Barbarians, so much respect did they pay to one another, even while contending for the victory.

But, not to wander too far, let us return to the affairs of GOD. The happiest person in the whole Assemblage was a poor Old Woman about eighty years of age, who in the eyes of Men seemed nearest to unhappiness. For a long while she had lost the use of her sight and, as she was unable to support herself during the short time she had still to live, she was compelled to follow her children wherever they went. The Name of GOD had never come to her ears; but, when the Holy Ghost wishes to take possession of a heart, it is soon won. This Woman took fire at hearing the first news of her Salvation. She was angry with herself for having remained all her life in ignorance of the Truths that we propounded to her. She detested her sins, asked for Baptism, and would think of nothing but Heaven; Father Claude Pijart baptized her. Such manifest joy appeared on her features that it was easy to see that GOD exerted a powerful influence on her heart. Thus she could not sufficiently congratulate herself of her happiness; and, to show how much she felt it, she tendered as a gift a Beaver skin, having nothing more valuable. But the Father refused it, being already amply repaid at seeing a Soul so soon prepared for Heaven.

In this gathering of so many assembled Nations, we strove to win the affections of the chief personages by means of feast and presents. In consequence of this, the Pauoitigoueieuhak invited us to go and see them in their own Country. (They are a Nation of the Algonquin Language, distant from the Hurons a hundred or a hundred and twenty leagues towards the West whom we call the Inhabitants of the Sault.) We promised to pay them a visit, to see how they might be disposed, in order to labour for their Conversion, especially as we learned that a more remote Nation whom they call Pouteatami had abandoned their own Country and taken refuge with the Inhabitants of the Sault, in order to remove from some other hostile Nation who persecuted them with endless wars. We selected Father Charles Raymbault to undertake this journey; and as, at the same time, some Hurons were to be of the party, Father Isaac Jogues was chosen, that he might deal with them."

It is somewhat unfortunate that the Jesuits were more interested in the spiritual than the geographical, for the "Bay of Lakes" might refer to Cache Bay, Callander Bay, Fish Bay, etc. However, the fact that the priest was on the beach watching the "snake" dance descend a neighbouring "Mountain" inclines me to think that Bourford Hill (i.e. the area of the Callander Lookout) was the location of this particular Feast.

In the sense that the different groups of Indians can be said to constitute different "nations," this Feast was an international event. Participants included the Hurons, Algonquins from the Ottawa Valley, and the Sauteurs ('Saut" or "Pauoitigoueiuhak) from the Lake Superior and Sault Ste. Marie area. In fact, this was the first meeting of the latter with the Jesuits. The French priests accepted an invitation to visit the Sauteurs, and later established the first mission at Sault Ste. Marie, a direct result of this Feast on Lake Nipissing. Another first resulted as well, but a much less happy one. During his ministries on Lake Nipissing in the summer of 1641 Father Raymbault began to debilitate. Despite this he followed the Sauteurs to Sault Ste. Marie in the summer of 1642 before returning to Quebec for proper care. But it was too late, and he died on October 22, 1642, the first Jesuit to die in Canada.

The feast had its athletic and competitive aspects. Prizes were awarded for physical strength, bodily skill and agility, with athletes obviously travelling great distances to compete. It is unfortunate that the missionaries did not discuss these competitions in more detail, but it is fun to speculate that a version of the Ontario Summer Games was held on Lake Nipissing more than three centuries ago.

More than anything else, however, this passage describes a religious festival. And the fact that the cultured Jesuits were impressed with the music would indicate that the ceremony possessed solemnity and dignity. Revealed here is the belief of the Nipissings in the life hereafter, their desire to put down the devil and their reverence for the dead — all associated with a feast dedicated to the zest for life.

We are not given any indication here how often the Nipissings held the ceremony of "The Feast of the Dead." The Feast of the Dead was held by most eastern tribes. The Five Nations who may have been the first to honour their dead in this manner held such ceremonies every ten to twelve years, each time it was necessary to move their village due to filth and unsanitary conditions that accumulated during this interval, as well as the decreased availability of firewood.

The Hurons held the feast more often. They also involved the recent dead at any stage of decomposition. They would strip the flesh from the skeleton and prepare the bones for the ceremony. It would appear that either the Nipissings did not involve the more recent dead, or had made these preparations previous to the arrival of the Jesuits.

The results of the "Feast of the Dead," and the burying of all the bones in communal grave, are the very graves that have been discovered elsewhere by archaeological digging and often reveal the location of early Indian villages. Undoubtedly there are several locations around the shores of Lake Nipissing where these communal graves do exist or have existed, but to my knowledge none have been discovered.

The illustration above is an artist's rendering of a 1717 sketch (artist unknown) in the Biblioteque Nationale, Paris, of a 'well dressed Nipissing Indian man' suggesting their possible cool weather attire.

Chapter 3

The Nipissing Way of Life

With Lalemant's writings of 1640 and 1642 close at hand, it would seem appropriate to describe more fully the Nipissings' way of life. It has already been established that they were nomadic hunters and traders. Their tribal and social organization reflected this activity.

Clans were made up of individuals claiming common ancestry. Two people from the same clan could not marry. The tribal chief was elected. His power was not great. The tribe divided into bands of closely related clans. It was the duty of the chief to regulate relations between bands and with other tribes. In peacetime his main job was to convene the tribal council to discuss important matters. In time of war his importance increased because it was he who planned strategy and led the tribe into battle.

Their main villages were made up of "cabins" of crude construction that could be raised or dismounted in a few hours. These "cabins" were the familiar birch bark wigwams. Although not as sophisticated as the Iroquoian long house, they had the advantage of being more portable, and far less smoky.

Their clothing naturally changed from season to season. In summer the children ran naked, the men wore breechcloths, and the women were fully covered. Often they would smear their bodies with grease as a protection against insects. In winter the garments were fashioned from fur, and leggings and sleeves were worn. Their feet were protected by buckskin moccasins. Before the arrival of the European with his variety of trade goods, the garments were sewn with the sinews of animals and needles of bone.

It was the women's work to dress skins, make clothing, attend to the hut, cut and gather firewood and prepare the meals. The cooking was done by heating stones and placing them into birch bark containers filled with water, scraps of meat or fish, and ground corn.

Hunter and warrior were the roles of the male. When not on these pursuits he was busy fashioning tools — making spearheads, carving paddles, and shaping bone or stone into skinning and scraping knives. Part of every encampment was a canoe frame, made by driving stakes into the ground. During the summer there seemed always to be a canoe at some stage of manufacture.

Common to all Algonquin tribes the Nipissing believed that the earth was populated by manitous or spirits. (Manitou could be either a good god or an evil devil depending on the context.) The chief spirit was the "Great Hare," known as "Michabo" or "Manibozko," the spirit who had created the world and who continued to control it. They believed in immortality of the soul. Awaiting the good, the generous and the courageous was the Happy Hunting ground, where game was abundant, and good health and agility of body was enjoyed by all. But for the cowardly, the selfish, and the evil, there was to be a land of snow and icy winds where they would wander forever, half starved and chilled to the bone.

During his stay on Lake Superior, Alexander Henry learned of the legend of the Great Hare. He recorded the following account.

> *Nanibozhu is otherwise called by the names of Minabojou, Michabou, Messou, Shactac, and a variety of others, but all of which the interpretation appears to be, The Great Hare. The traditions, related of the Great Hare, are as varied as his name. He was represented to me as the founder, and indeed creator, of the Indian nations of North America. He lived originally toward the going down of the sun, where being warned, in a dream, that the inhabitants would be drowned by a general flood, produced by heavy rains, he built a raft, on which he afterward preserved his own family, and all the animal world without exception. According to his dream, the rains fell, and a flood ensued. His raft drifted for many moons, during which no land was discovered. His family began to despair of a termination to the calamity; and the animals, who had then the use of speech, murmured loudly against him. In the end, he produced a new earth, placed the animals upon it, and created man.*

> *At a subsequent period, he took from the animals the use of speech. This act of severity was performed in consequence of a conspiracy, into which they had entered against the human race. At the head of the conspiracy was the bear; and the great increase which had taken place among the animals rendered their numbers formidable. I have heard many other stories concerning Nanibozhu, and many have been already given to the public; and this at least is certain, that sacrifices are offered, on the island, which is called his grave or tumulus, by all who pass it. I landed there, and found on the projecting rocks a quantity of tobacco, rotting in the rain together with kettles, broken guns and a variety of other articles. His spirit is supposed to make this its constant residence; and here to preside over the lake, and over the Indians, in their navigation and fishing.*

Of the names here given, Messou was that used among the Quebec Montagnais and other Algonkian tribes of the east. The form occurs frequently in the early Jesuit Relations. Shactac is apparently a form of the Cree "Wisakketchak," which also appears in the Nipissing, "Wisakedjak."

The story of Nanibozhu is widespread among the western Algonkian peoples, who delight in the narration "of the deeds and exploits of the hero-god who figures in their creation and deluge legends, who taught them many arts and inventions, and who sometimes deceived them as well as helped them." The relation of these form a permanent source of pleasure around the fire during the long winter nights, and though later local surroundings have somewhat coloured the older story, yet in the main, it is alike in all branches of the great Algonquin nation. The hero bears a close analogy to Napiu of the Blackfeet and Gluskey of the Micmacs.

To the early French missionaries, the Nipissing were also known as "Gens Sorcier" or the "Sorcerers". This appellation was applied because they appeared to have far more "medicine men" throughout their tribe, than most others. The Jesuits said, "These Sorcerers — it is thus the French call that tribe, because they make special professions of consulting their Manitou, or talking to the devil." Juggling and gymnastics made up part of their worship. Neighbouring tribes were so convinced that the Nipissings could inflict evil at remote distances that they crossed their territory with trepidation and loaded with gifts of appeasement.

During Champlain's first trip up the Ottawa River, he sat in council with the Algonquins of Alumette Island, addressing Chief Tessouat. "The object of my journey," he said, "is to assure you of my affection, and of my desire to aid you in your wars. It is my desire to visit the nation of the Nipissings, who dwell six days journey to the west. I wish to invite them to go on the warpath. I request of you four canoes and a crew of eight men to make this expedition."

The elders smoked sullenly and muttered to one another. Tessouat, after thanking Champlain for his consideration, spoke: "Now as for the proposal to push westward and visit the Nipissing, we advise against it. The way is hard. Those tribes are sorcerers; they have killed many of my people by magic and poisoning."

Great store was put in the interpretation of dreams. Shamans specially appointed and trained to interpret dreams were common throughout the Nipissing villages.

An example of this practice may have taken place in the autumn of 1649. Old Artitook had been a Nipissing sorcerer for most of his seventy years. He had been head medicine man for the past five years. Many young braves had applied to apprentice under his tutorship. The tuition fee was dear, months were spent in isolation, deep in the forest, and the student practiced meditation, juggling and philosophizing on the interpretation of dreams.

The Nipissing required a séance of their seers regularly, but would demand one when things did not seem right or news was not forthcoming from outside sources.

The summer of 1649 carried an ominous air; therefore a séance was ordered in August of that year.

As was the custom, Artitook chose a young teenage virgin. Her mind had to be clear of worldly pleasures. Likewise he chose a young boy whose purity could also be vouched for. These two young people were chosen at the first new moon. They were chosen for the purpose of dreaming.

Their dreams, dreamed under deep sleep, without inhibition, translated by an expert like Artitook, would tell of present situations blended into future insights.

The Nipissings chose specific locations for various religious ceremonies. As with all Algonquin people some areas would be considered taboo, while others were considered sacred. The choices of these locations were probably deeply rooted in past experiences of the tribe or had been customary. Perhaps some were located, in isolation, close to the main routes of travel. These sites may have been strategically placed, in an attempt to cast evil spells on intruders entering the domain of the Nipissings.

Let us suppose that one such site was located at the west end of Trout Lake, just west of the travelled portion of the lake, that is from the La Vase portages, out of Dugas Bay and on down the main lake. This site would be free from the prying eyes of the traveller, and isolated from the main body of the tribe on Lake Nipissing. Shamans and dreamers had used this site for many generations.

Artitook didn't know of its origin. This site had been quite elaborately constructed, elaborate to the semi-nomadic Nipissings, anyway, who left very few signs of their comings and goings.

A quiet cove, fringed by a semi-circular beach, had been chosen for this sacred site. About 150 feet from the beach the land rose into granite gneiss mounds and ridges, one of these mounds rising 30 feet above the surrounding terrain. The face of this mound had been denuded of foliage. From the summit a set of stone stairs was carefully built to the base of the mound. On either side of the mound stairs were also built, and these three stairs joined at the summit forming an arch. The stairs were walled a few feet high by inlaid rocks. The summit was Dreamer's Rock.

To this site came the old shaman, Artitook, the two young dreamers, and six understudies of the shaman, who would assist and learn.

Wigwams were set up just inside the treeline of the beach.

The dreamers and the medicine man would fast for five days and nights. The understudies would look after their needs. During the period of fasting, the understudies would make ready Dreamer's Rock. This was done by sweeping the steps bare of decaying pine needles and leaves, being very careful not to disturb the lichen-covered rocks making up the side walls.

Pictographs were etched on these rocks that portrayed past dream experiences that could be interpreted only by a full-fledged medicine man.

They also prepared the dreamer's bower, at the summit. This was done by placing small balsam boughs on the rock, butt end down. After placing several hundred in an area 6 x 3 feet, workers produced a springy mattress Two such beds were made.

On top of these mattresses they placed luxurious robes of prime beaver and otter skins.

On the sixth morning a huge feast of boiled dog meat was served to the old sorcerer and dreamers only. (The eastern Indian kept dogs for religious ceremonies and feasts only. Surprising as it may seem he never used them for hunting or as beasts of burden. The use of the animal as a sled dog was copied from the white man, not the Eskimo. The Indian has used them for this purpose only in the last 100 years or so, in spite of the fact that the coureur de bois and the voyageur had used sled dogs for 200 hundred years previously.)

The two dreamers had been denied sleep for 48 hours, before the dog meat feast. They were escorted to the summit of Dreamer's Rock to the awaiting beds. The boy dreamer was led up the left-hand staircase, and the girl up the right.

The old shaman ascended the centre stairs. Very little gesticulation was required by Artitook until the pair were in deep sleep. They would be allowed to sleep for 24 hours.

An almost airtight skin tent had been prepared for the old shaman on the sand beach. The tent was four feet by four feet and about six feet high. He would spend the next 24 hours in this cubicle, conjuring, ranting, raving, sweating, shaking and generally making himself fit to interpret any dream the dreamers would relate to him on their descent. Artitook entered the tent naked; the only utensil with him was a waterproof birch bark container half full of fresh lake water.

The understudies heated stones in a large perpetual fire on the beach. The old shaman would receive these stones in his bare hands and drop them sizzling into the bark water container.

He was chanting in Algonquin, and then he would give long discourses in a language unfamiliar to the understudies. This was the tongue of the sorcerer, a vocabulary they would learn before graduation.

After a few hours his tent began shaking violently, so much so that it would rise off the ground a few inches. This was too much for the youngest novice; he peeked through a crevice in the tent. The old Shaman was chanting with arms outstretched above his head. The shaking of the tent was from no other cause than the spirits themselves, so the young understudies were convinced.

The dreamers had been sleeping 12 hours when three of the understudies placed the Nipissing totems beside them, a freshly killed blue heron, an unskinned beaver, a red squirrel and a roll of birch bark. These totems would cause the dreams to be true and accurate.

On the morning of the seventh day old Artitook emerged from the shaking tent, glistening with sweat. He waded straight into the lake, dove under, rubbed himself and returned to the shore. He dressed in his buckskins and sat on a log in the shade and calmly awaited the return of the dreamers.

The dreamers were awake by now and summoned to return to the lakeshore by their three attendants. They were both led from the summit by the central staircase, a ritual practiced from generations past with no apparent meaning. As soon as the girl dreamer saw the old sorcerer, she cried out "Wawa, Wawa, Wawa!" Old Artitook calmed her, sat her in the shade and asked her to slowly recall her dreams. "Wawa!" she again exclaimed. "What about the geese?" asked the old shaman.

The girl blinked her eyes and finally realized that she was awake and back in the world of reality and began to narrate her dream.

"Hundreds of black geese were flying north, they crossed a large frozen river, and the end of a large lake partly covered with ice. I had never seen pure black geese before and did not know why the geese would be flying north when all the lakes and streams were ice-covered and all the forest was a blanket of snow.

"As I was contemplating this the main flock of geese veered to the northwest and continued on across swamp lands, rivers and lakes. They were flying very high, the weather was still and very sunny, the visibility seemed unlimited.

"The flock was approaching the shore of a very large lake. The shoreline of this large lake was occupied by an extremely large flock of white geese, many thousands. The black geese landed beside the flock of white ones. Then my dream became fuzzy, but I do remember that the feet of the black geese seemed to turn into snowshoes as they landed. The next I remember is that the black geese took to flight, landed a few miles in from the coast, and seemed to descend straight into the thick forest.

"After the black geese left there were very many dead white ones. I saw patches of blood all over the snow, many dead geese with red blood trickling down their white feathers. That was the end of my dream."

The boy dreamer, who had been segregated from the girl while she narrated her dream, was brought to the presence of Artitook.

"And you my son, what did you dream?" asked the old sorcerer.

The boy thought for a few minutes, trying to recall images that were not too clear. "Now I remember," he said, "there were very many mink, maybe a hundred or more, swimming up a large river. I know the river!" he exclaimed, as if he had an instant recall. "It was the same river that I paddled down, just this spring, in the bow of my father's canoe, when we went to trade with the French at Quebec."

"Were the mink swimming up the Ottawa River?" quizzed the old shaman.

"Yes" said the boy. "It was the Ottawa River. They swam very fast; they swam up the rapids and up falls without slowing down. When they came to the mouth of the Mattawa River, they did not hesitate, but turned west and came straight up the Mattawa. And still they came through the fast water and rapids with no difficulty. It seemed that they were coming straight for this very spot, yet they didn't. They didn't pass Talon Chutes, I'm sure. I did not see them pass through that white water. Instead they climbed out on the riverbank. It was in the fall, the trees had turned to red, orange and yellow, yet when these mink crawled onto the shore they were immediately covered in snow. That's funny, that's all I remember."

Old Artitook stood up and addressed his understudies, "Let us return to Lake Nipissing to warn the Chief — the Iroquois are on the warpath."

There are disappointingly few Indian legends existing among the Nipissings today. I have heard of the taboo of the Manitou Islands, for example, since my arrival in North Bay, but have been unable to find any historical reference to it.

Ernest Couchie, an elder of the Nipissing Reserve, feels that the superstition started long ago, by eerie sounds made, by water rushing through caverns that have eroded underwater against the walls of the island. This explanation of course was unavailable to the Indians who camped there, and they assumed the sounds to be the work of evil spirits. From this, he says, the taboo developed. At Dokis Bay, Gordon Restoule, who is currently researching his tribal history, tells the story of a haunted island. It is not clear that this island was in the French River or Lake Nipissing, but the story could easily have been originally associated with one of the Manitou Islands. Perhaps this story, coupled with Ernie Couchie's explanation, is the answer to the Manitou taboo. The following is the story told by Gordon Restoule.

A long time ago (circa 1650) a beautiful Nipissing maiden named Snow Bird, daughter of a chief, voluntarily left her family's hearth and wigwam with a handsome Iroquois brave, who was of course an enemy. The chief and a few hand-picked Nipissing braves pursued the pair. [The pursuit probably took place across the La Vase portage since it is likely that the young Iroquois would be taking his new love back to the safety of the Iroquois fortification at Pimissi Bay.]

Somewhere en route they were captured. The Iroquois was dragged back to Lake Nipissing for torture and death. Snow Bird received a tongue lashing from her father the chief. On an island on Lake Nipissing the Iroquois brave was burned at the stake. [No doubt an island was chosen for the punishment of the Iroquois lover, in the event that his comrades might try to take them by surprise].

The maiden, who was required to watch the torture, suddenly jumped into the fire, flinging her arms around her dying lover, and she also met the same fate.

If you happen to camp for the night, on Haunted Island, you can still hear the screams of the Nipissing maiden as she jumps into the fire.

The following legend has been passed down from generation to generation in the Nipissing band, and no one knows of its origin. The story was passed on to me by Lawrence Commanda, a Nipissing Indian living in North Bay.

Again note the historic accuracy contained in this legend re: The Iroquois wars. The legend of course is inaccurate as far as the fort at the Mouth of the Sturgeon River is concerned, which did not exist in the same period as the Iroquois wars. (1650).

The Legend of The Manitous

It is generally assumed by those interested in the legend of the Manitous that the story is referring to the group of islands on Lake Nipissing, because of the plural Manitous. Actually, the expression in Ojibway "minito-n-goong" refers only to one island, the largest of the group on the lake. Because it is on this island that the legend's incidents were to have taken place. Two facets that are important in the legend are:

    1. Witchcraft as it was practiced in that period, and

    2. The Indian wars that were going on at that time.

Two important battles were supposed to have been fought in this area. One was near the mouth of Chippewa Creek, the other was near the outlet of Lake Talon.

It was the presence of the Iroquois that sent the small group of Indians to the largest of the group of islands on the lake now known as Nipissing (Nbi-seeng) to depend completely on the wildlife and fish off the lake to sustain life to the small group. This continued for most of the winter till the wildlife diminished and the lake froze over,

Because so much is lost in the translation, it is well to first acquaint you with the witchcraft as it was practiced in that period of time. The small band was without a seer or one who practiced witchcraft so they went about making one. This they did by isolating one of the children and putting her on a 21 day fast. At the end of that period she would know the power she would have. An eleven-year-old girl was selected to fast as this was the desired age.

As the girl was finishing her time of fasting, food ran out completely in the camp. The other children used to come and see the little girl in her hut every day. On this particular day one of the older children was sent to get water from the water hole in the small lake that was on the island. While the child was drawing the water he noticed a fish — a sturgeon, a large one — in the water hole. He ran home hurriedly to tell the adults what he had seen. The elders went to the waterhole, caught the fish, cooked it, and ate some of it. As the day wore on the girl in isolation began to wonder why her younger brother and sister hadn't come to visit her. She thought she could hear moans coming from the camp so she ventured out. First she saw depressions in the fresh snow. They all led to the waterhole in the pond, and they all came from the tepees, and some came from her father's house.

Next she went to her father's house, and as she peered into the gloom of the house and her eyes became accustomed to the darkness, a huge snake took shape in the far side of the room, asleep on the floor. She gazed around the room, and there on the other side of the room her father lay; the upper part of his torso was still intact but his lower part had turned into a huge snake. Parts of the sturgeon were still in the cooking pot, and when the father saw her he began to speak to her saying, "Do not eat any of the fish, it has been poisoned." Pointing to the reptile on the floor on the far side of the room he continued, "Go, leave this place before your mother awakens and your brother and sisters return, they will surely eat you. Go to the fort near the mouth of the Sturgeon River. There you will find a group of our people. Tell them what you have seen and what has happened here on this island. No one will ever be able to live here; this place is cursed. Hurry now and leave this place."

So the eleven-year-old girl set out on the long trek to the fort near the mouth of the Sturgeon River. There she told the band of Indians at the fort of her experience on the island.

With food and extra clothing a party of Indians went out the next morning to the island to see what happened to the band of Indians and what could be done for them. What they saw was exactly as the little girl had told them. No one in the camp — the only signs were the deep slimy depressions in the freshly fallen snow. These all came from the tepees and led into the waterhole in the pond on the island.

This is 1970: until now no one has lived on the island. Many years have passed since those incidents were supposed to have happened. The characters in the legend may never have existed. Yet with each telling of the legend the same questions arise. Did a small band of Indians really live on the island? And did an eleven-year-old child really make the long trek in the late winter many years ago to tell a bizarre tale of seeing her family turn into reptiles. It is true that the island is big enough for cottage sites. There is ideal fishing in the area, yet to this day no one has lived on the island any length of time. And as long as no one lives there, to the Indians who are acquainted with the legend, the curse still remains on the island...

All peoples everywhere have speculated upon the mystery of creation, and the Nipissings were no exception. In the following

THE LEGEND of THE MANITOUS.

passage from The Jesuit Relations, a Jesuit and his interpreter, Jean Nicolet, discuss this mystery with an Algonkian Indian, who is evidently a member of the Nipissing Tribe.

Father Buteux entered a Cabin with Sieur Nicolet, who understands the Algonquin tongue very well. An Algonquin, who acts the part of a Wiseacre, invited them to sit down near him, which they did. And thereupon he told them that the Savages recognized two Manitous; but, for his part, he recognized a third, who presided over war. That one of the three had made the land, at least, that of his country; as to that of the French, he was not entirely certain. Having made the land he produced the animals and all other things of this country. The narrator gave him a great lake, or a waterfall, for his home, as we give the sea to Neptune. This worthy creator of the earth, drawing his bow one day upon a Beaver, to chase it far away, in order to people the country with them, missed it; and the arrow lodging in a tree, had made it very beautiful and smooth; and as for this not being true, "I have, "he said, "known old men who have seen this tree." He related a thousand other foolish tales. The Father had asked him where this God was before he created the earth." In his Canoe," he replied, "which was floating upon the waters." "If he had a Canoe," was asked to him, "there must have been trees, for it is made of the bark of trees; if there were trees, there was land; if there was land, how has he created it?" "The Land," he replied, "was there before, but it was flooded by a deluge." "And before the deluge, who created this land?" "I know nothing about it; you have more intelligence than I have, do not ask me anything more." "Since thou dost not know it, listen to us," was said to him. "If I were young, you would be right in wishing to teach me; but as I am already old, you would lose your pains, for I have no longer any memory." "It is because thou art old," said the interpreter, "that thou must hasten to learn these truths; for, if thou dost not believe, thou wilt be very unhappy after thy death." Thereupon he outlined for him the creation of the world, redemption, and the punishments and rewards of the other life. "I have not," said he, "the mind to be able to retain so many things; teach them to the children, who have a good memory." Nevertheless, this doctrine made some impression upon his mind; for since then he has taught some sick persons what he could remember of it.

Authors Note: The following tribal laws, which were supposedly those incorporated by the Eastern Algonquin Nation, were probably known by the Nipissings who were a part of this large nation. The origin of these laws, or their actual use, is unknown. To what extent the Nipissings adhered to them is also unknown. At any rate I am introducing them here for the reader's interest.

Tribal Laws of the Eastern Algonquin

THE CHILDREN OF LIGHT

1 Condemn Not A Man by the hue of his flesh, the lilt of his voice or the curvature of his face, for it is within him and unseen that which can love you.

2 Look into the eyes of your child once a moon and see there for you the miracle of the Great Spirit.

3 He who knows not the love of a small child cannot know the love of the Great Spirit.

4 When you think you are a great chief and above your tribesmen go into the forest, stand before a mighty pine, then tell that pine how great a man you really are.

5 If you find fear in your heart go into the mountains, stand high on the peak, watch the storm come from the horizon, see the lightning and hear the thunder and know that all this power is small in comparison to the power of the Great Spirit with which he has to protect you.

6 When you become a wolf in the lodge of your loved ones go into the forest, find the tranquility, there rest a while, then come home again, a man.

7 Beware of the man that smiles too soon, for does not the wolf smile just before he bites?

8 Father in your youth have time for your son and in your age your son shall have time for you.

9 In the profusion of the forest examine the small weed and note there the work of the Great Spirit.

10 Sing loud in the forest and be not ashamed of your voice, for the Great Spirit loves the song of the Raven, and did he not give him his?

11 Hurt not any child for they are the possessions of the Great Spirit and remain so until maturity.

12 Honour your father and your child shall honour you.

13 Make sure others are not hungry when you have sufficient for loneliness will drive you mad.

14 Remember, hate destroys the hater and the hated watches him die.

15 Mend the tribe you have defeated in war and they shall no longer be your enemies.

16 If a stranger enter your lodge, feed first his dog, and by this he will know you are of a kind heart.

17 Gratitude comes from the heart, and the heart cannot speak.

18 Knock not upon the lodge of another for you may frighten the children.

19 Make sure the smell of your people is a good smell to your nostrils.

20 When you take of the trees of the forest thank the Great Spirit, for they were made by him and given to you as to your need.

21 The Shaman Chief shall kill no game, for his duty is to preserve all life of the tribe and pertaining to the tribe.

22 If the Dog Soldier be commanded by the chief to take the life of another, the chief is responsible and may only do so in the defence of the tribe or the chieftainship.

23 When you walk on the land of a strange tribe, remove your moccasins in honour of this tribe, for their land is their great love and the possession of their God.

24 If you wish to feel the hand of the Great Spirit stand naked in the sun.

25 Clothe yourself for warmth and not for shame.

26 Love is man's greatest possession, for even the beasts of the forest will return it when loaned.

27 Despise not the infirmity of your brother's mind or body or any condition of life for they may become in time your own lot.

28 When sickness or infirmity or the reverses of fortune affect us, the sincerity of friendship is found.

29 The path to the Great Spirit is as wide to the tribesman as it is to the chiefs.

30 To discover truth the mind must be sedate, seek council at the council rock.

31 In all your reason employ your mind in the search of truth.

32 The true worship of the Great Spirit is an important and reverent necessity to success.

33 Know that to be a leader and a chief you must be the servant of the least of your people.

34 Know that the Great Spirit is the light beyond the sun, who created the sun, water and earth, then with these things he created a man.

35 The eldest of the lodge is chief of the lodge and though he becomes feeble, you in time will be also.

36 If your father's bones lie in the land, you are of the land, for his spirit lies with the spirits of this land.

37 It shall be the father who counsels in truth with his son in matters of the flesh, and mothers with their daughters. Sons belong to fathers for they were once sons, and daughters to mothers, for they were once daughters. The son raised by a mother will never become a warrior, and a daughter raised by a father shall have difficulty in the search for gentleness.

38 If your village stinks, sickness will visit your people.

39 Make no dung or water within four lengths of a man, to a river, lake or brook.

40 If a man be crippled or maimed, it is the will of the Great Spirit. Never condemn the will of the Great Spirit.

41 Feed the stranger who appears at your lodge, for he is also a child of the Great Spirit.

42 Beware of the man who has no love for his dog, particularly if his dog has no love for him.

43 If you see a man unclothed in the sun, know that it is beautiful, for it is the likeness of the Great Spirit.

44 Know that flesh upon flesh is a very small part of love and that it is the completion and not the beginning.

45 Take for yourself one mate and you shall have peace in your lodge.

46 The child of the elk and the deer is owned by neither.

47 The man who touches a deer and lets it live is truly a hunter, but he who kills for the like of killing has a lack of heart and few friends.

48 If you wish to hunt for the sake of killing, hunt a man, he is your equal and can fire back the arrow.

49 Tend the wounds of your brother, for the Great Spirit made both of you in the same manner.

50 If it be necessary to punish a child, do it in such a way as to improve his strength or his mind, but lay not your hand upon him for you may damage the possession of your god, his gift to you.

51 Know the success of a man by the weight of his child and the smile

upon his child's face.

52 Blame no child how it came to be, for the gift of life is from the Great Spirit.

53 When the nose of your son reaches your first rib, take him into the forest, kill for him a deer; from the foreshoulders to the rear, remove one hand span by two arm lengths of leather, then from the underside remove a strip the width of your thumb long enough to circle his waist; put the warm hide between his legs and lace it through the belt, front and back. He will then know the reason for killing; waste not the remainder of the deer.

54 Hold your head high my son for it is your father you honour. If you cannot honour your father, you will never hold your head high.

55 The evil of nudity is generally in the eye of the beholder.

56 Humility is one of the most amiable virtues one can possess.

57 The child who is solemnly fed and never injured in games of hunt, or damaged from childish play, will become like a beast of prey who destroys without pity, for the search for the knowledge of suffering.

58 Flattery made to deceive and betray should be avoided as a rabid wolf.

59 Unhappiness is brought to those who are deaf to the calls of duty and of honour.

60 If you have only trees to view, you have many possessions.

61 They who have much given to them will have much to answer for.

62 It is not to be expected that those who in early life have been dark and deceitful should afterwards become fair and ingenuous.

63 They who have laboured to make us wise and good are the persons whom we ought to love and respect and whom we ought to be grateful to.

64 From the character of those whom you associate with, your own will be estimated.

65 It is the Great Spirit who breathes the wind upon the earth with the breath of Spring who covers it with splendour and beauty.

66 When the trees get their leaves, the brook again sings after the long winter, and the land becomes green again, it is the time of giving.

67 The truest gift in substance your child can give you is two sticks tied together; it is not the two sticks, it is the tying.

68 To enjoy your own land, look back upon it from another.

69 The ruin of a tribe is generally preceded by a universal degeneracy of manners and contempt toward the Great Spirit.

70 We are frequently benefited by what we have dreaded.

71 It is no great virtue to live lovingly with good-natured and meek persons.

72 It deserves our best skill to inquire into those rules by which we may guide our judgement.

73 If we lay no restraint upon our lust, no control upon our appetites and passions, they will hurry us to guilt and misery.

74 To promote iniquity in others is the same as being the actors of it ourselves.

75 Be not afraid of the wicked, they are under the control of providence.

76 Consciousness of guilt may justly affright us.

77 Convey unto others no intelligence that you would be ashamed to avow.

78 How many disappointments have in their consequences saved a man from ruin and his Chieftainship.

79 A well-poised mind makes a cheerful countenance.

80 Virtue embalms the memory of good.

81 The Shaman may dispense but the Great Spirit alone can bless it.

82 Condemn not a man till you have walked a mile in his moccasins.

83 In many pursuits we embark with pleasure and land sorrowfully.

84 Rocks, mountains and caverns are of indispensable use both to the earth and to man.

85 The hive of the village or the lodge is in the best condition when there is the least buzz in it.

86 The roughness found on our entrance into the paths of virtue and learning, grow smoother as we advance into manhood.

87 The harmlessness of many animals and the enjoyment that they have of life, should plead for them against cruel usage.

88 We are often very busy to no useful purpose.

89 Genuine charity, how liberal so ever it may be, will never impoverish ourselves.

90 However disagreeable, we must resolutely perform our duty.

91 A bout of sickness is often a kind of chastisement and discipline, to moderate the affection for the things of this life.

92 Health and peace, our most valuable possessions, are obtained at a small price.

93 True happiness is an enemy to pomp and noise.

94 Few depressions are more distressing than those that we make upon ourselves in our own ingratitude.

95 Cultivate your own heart and not that of evil ways.

96 Wars are attended with distasteful and devastating affects; it is confessedly the scourge of our angry passion.

97 The blood of all men when spilled together cannot be defined apart.

98 Encourage no man to do what he believes to be wrong.

99 It shall not be said that we are charitable donors when our deeds proceed with selfish motives.

100 A great joy to a father is the glint of the sweat on the muscles of his son in worthy effort.

101 The gentleness of a daughter is a joy to her mother.

102 Endeavour to become a great chief and you stand a good chance of becoming a great warrior.

103 Great warriors do not always fight, but with wisdom, are peacemakers.

104 May a young man put his hand in the hand of an old man and let him live again a day of his youth, and from this learning your youth will become more keenly full.

105 Do one great deed in your life and it will be easier to die.

106 Recompense to no man evil for evil; this will define the leaders of men for the chieftains of the tribe.

107 Meekness controls our angry passions, candour our severe judgements.

108 To be faithful among the faithless argues great grants of principle.

109 Be not fooled but know that wars are regulated robberies.

110 A friend exaggerates a man's virtues, an enemy enflames his crimes

111 A witty and humorous vein more often produces enemies.

112 Many have been visited with afflictions who have not profited by them.

113 The experience of want enhances the virtue of plenty.

114 The wicked are often ensnared in the trap they lay for others.

115 When retiring at the setting of the day and there is an argument in your lodge, say you are wrong, though you are right, and go to bed happy.

116 It is hard to say what diseases are controllable; they are all under the controls of the Great Spirit.

117 Fear not the Shaman for he is guided by the Great Spirit, and his cures are the gifts of the Great Spirit's forest.

118 A steady mind may receive council, but there is no hold on a changeable humour.

119 Excessive merriment is the path to grief.

120 To practice virtue is a sure way to love it.

121 One should study to live peaceably with all men.

122 A great warrior has a soul that can secretly defy death and consider it nature's privilege to die.

123 The man who claims no fear is an idiot and a liar.

124 Let not the sternness of virtue affright us; she will soon become amiable.

125 True valour protects the feeble and humbles the oppressor.

126 Hurt no child or elder in war for they are the possessions of the Great Spirit.

127 One should recollect that however favourable we may appear to ourselves, we are vigorously examined by others.

128 Virtue can render youth, as well as old age, honour.

129 Rumour most often tells false tales.

130 Let gossip not break a treaty between friends or tribes; often a jealous tongue will use it to dishonourable advantage.

131 Weak minds are ruffled by trifling things.

132 It is an honourable chieftain who feeds the hungry, visits the sick and clothes the naked and helpless of his children.

133 It is good to be cheerful without levity.

134 The gaiety of youth should be tempered with the respect of age.

135 The most acceptable sacrifice is that of a humble and contrite heart.

136 We are accountable for whatever we patronize in others.

137 It is a mark of a vicious disposition to torture animals, to make them smart and agonize for our devotion.

138 A guilty man cannot avoid many melancholy apprehensions.

139 If we injure others we must expect retaliation.

140 The conscious receiver is as bad as the thief.

141 The Great Spirit is not only the creator but the ruler and preserver of all life.

142 Honest endeavours, if persevered in, will finally be successful.

143 It requires a kind heart as well as a just mind to be a great chief.

144 Inquire into the cause of the crimes of your warriors before you pass judgement on the crime itself.

145 If your warrior steals a loaf of bread, judge him for why. If to feed his children, you are also responsible as Chief that no child should be hungry, but if for self-gain only, then he is guilty.

146 When the father of a child be a slave to your tribe, remember the child is yet the possession of the Great Spirit who at the time of maturity may claim your tribe as his own; this be his right.

147 There be first the child, then the rabbit warrior, then the claim to the tribe at maturity, then the hunter, then the dog soldier (the protector of children and the chieftainship), then a councillor, then an elder.

148 The bloodline chief becomes in line for chieftainship, being the youngest son at the death of the grandfather; therefore the father chief will have time to train him.

149 The child will choose the parents upon the death of his own.

150 Children in their childish battles must be taught to feed the loser for the following day.

151 Learning is losing an argument.

Chapter 4

The Iroquois Wars

When Champlain first penetrated the North American continent in the summer of 1609 in the company of some Algonquin Indians, he fired on the Mohawk enemies of his travelling companions on the shore of what is now Lake Champlain. This was the first experience that the Iroquois had had with European firepower. It is often said that this one musket shot created enmity between the French and the powerful Five Nations Confederacy, and that the Five Nations never forgot the incident for over 150 years. This explanation of the French-Iroquois rivalry is appealing because it is so straightforward. But it is too simple. Rather, the French, in their quest for wealth in America discovered the value of the fur trade, and their location on the St. Lawrence River led them naturally into a trading alliance with the Hurons. This Iroquoian speaking group had resisted inclusion in the Five Nations Confederacy, and from their base at Huronia had, long before the French reached the new world, established commercial relations with their Algonquin neighbours. Their organization permitted them to secure the furs that the French wanted, and the French in turn were quite willing to let the Hurons occupy this middleman trading position between the interior tribes and the French.

The Five Nations, usually referred to collectively as the Iroquois, performed a similar service for the Dutch who established themselves at New Amsterdam (New York) and at Fort Orange (Albany). The long-standing Huron-Iroquois rivalry continued, but did not become intense until the 1640s when the supplies of furs in the Iroquois country began to run low. In that decade the Iroquois conducted a series of attacks and raids against the French and Huron trading routes and settlements, but the Hurons were more than able to hold their own in these skirmishes. In 1649, however, a strong and desperate offensive began, and in the end the Huron tribal and trading organization was destroyed. This story has been told many times, and most readers will be familiar with the accounts of the invasion and destruction of Huronia, and with the martyrdom of Jesuits like Fathers Jean de Brebeuf and Gabriel Lalemant. In this study attention will be directed on the effects of the Iroquois attacks on the trading partners of the Hurons, and especially on the Nipissings. And it was logical that the Iroquois would direct their venom against these people as well, for the contest was largely one of trading competition, and the Nipissings

Father Jean de Brebeuf

This is an artist's rendering of an undated painting by an unknown artist (La Ville Maison des Jesuites, Sillery, Quebec) including a detail (inset) from the 1665 painting "The Jesuit Martyrs," by Abbe Hugues Pommier (L'Hotel-Dieu, Quebec), based on Father Bressani's first-hand accounts of Iroquois torture.

played an important role in the overall structure of the Huron trading system.

The Iroquois did not launch these attacks from their home villages in New York State, but rather actually occupied the vacant territory surrounding their enemy, by building fortifications, living off the land, and occasionally receiving reinforcements from home. Within a year and a half all the Indians living on the French route of travel (Georgian Bay, French River, Lake Nipissing, the Mattawa and Ottawa), including 30,000 Hurons, were either killed or completely driven away.

The incredibility of a comparatively few invaders causing so much fear and havoc among their seemingly well-populated enemy can be explained by what I think is one of the best descriptions of the Iroquois torture that I have come across. An account of it has been given first-hand by the priest who received this torture and, God knows how, survived. The man involved was Father Francisco Bressani, an Italian Jesuit who, prior to the following ordeal, had visited the homelands of the Nipissings. He was therefore undoubtedly the first Italian to visit this region and to cross Lake Nipissing.

The cruelty of the Iroquois to prisoners was a spectre that moved step for step with every wilderness traveler. The other tribes practiced torture, but never with the diabolical and obscene imaginativeness employed by the Iroquois.

> *I know not whether Your Paternity will recognize the letter of a poor cripple, who formerly, when in perfect health, was well known to you. The letter is badly written, and quite soiled, because, in addition to other inconveniences, he who writes it has only one whole finger on his right hand; and it is difficult to avoid staining the paper with the blood which flows from his wounds, not yet healed: he uses arquebus powder for ink, and the earth for a table. He writes it from the country of the Iroquois.*

Thus the Jesuit, Francesco Bressani, began his first report on his captivity to the Father General of the Order in Europe, a letter that did not leave the Iroquois country, however, until the author himself had been ransomed by some kindly Dutch. At this point he did not mention that there were no whole fingers at all on his left hand, nor that the toes had been twisted from his feet; those details come to light, almost in casual mention, as his modest narrative proceeds with a detachment of statement that gives fresh perspective both to cruelty and man's ability to accept pain. In many ways Bressani's experience was unique, due as much to the quality of his mind, perhaps, as to Iroquois caprice. As Isaac Jogues had been two years earlier, Bressani was captured with his party on the St. Lawrence by Mohawks while on his way up to the Huron missions in the spring of 1644. Like Jogues, he too did not die under the tortures that fell to his lot, though his lasted nearly twice as long. He was taken on the twenty-seventh of April; the date of his letter to the Father General was July 15, and though the Iroquois had decided on the nineteenth of June to spare his life, his wounds still ran and he crouched in the shadow of death. He did not suffer immediate mutilation of his hands as Jogues had on the night after his capture — it was the favourite Iroquois preliminary torment — but he was made to watch while they cut up the body of a Christian Huron, boiled it, and ate it. Then they loaded him with packs he could barely stagger under and drove him barefoot through the snowy April woods, beating him whenever he faltered or failed to understand their orders and mocking him with details of the death they had in store for him.

On the upper Hudson, 18 days after he had been taken, the party came upon a fishing camp of 400 Iroquois. It marked the beginning of serious torture. They stripped him naked, and as they led him toward the camp of little huts, he saw for the first time the double line of the gauntlet — what Father Jogues had called "the narrow way of Paradise" — men, women, and children, all clamouring with rage or furious laughter, and armed with clubs, iron rods, thorny branches to flog the prisoners as they passed through.

Bressani was the first to enter the line, preceded and followed by an Iroquois so that he could not run; but he had hardly taken a step when a young brave confronted him and taking his left hand drove a knife between the third and little finger with such force that the hand was nearly split. He was covered with blood and heavily dazed when he emerged at the far end of the gauntlet, and had to be led through the cabins to the torture scaffold in the centre of the camp.

This, with the fires burning before it, was the symbol of dread that every forest wanderer carried with him wherever he might travel. "My heart shaked with trembling and fear, which took away my stomach," wrote Pierre Esprit Radisson, who as a youth had been tortured in a Mohawk village and had watched many other captives slowly put to death. The scaffold was a platform of bark raised five or six feet above the ground so that all could watch the prisoner's contortions. Through it rose the posts to which the prisoner was bound with strips of bark, sometimes a single post to which he was tied hand and foot, sometimes two posts, over which his arms were passed and bound by the forearms, which left the rest of his body free "to dance" and later, as they came to learn more of Christianity, the Iroquois sometimes used a cross. Here the prisoner, man or woman, was made to sing; war songs if he was a warrior, or such feeble defiance as a woman might find to utter, but which in any case the torturers, with grave attention to the niceties of pain, tried to reduce to wails of agony, and generally succeeded.

Yet there were many who endured everything without giving way. Such was Bressani, a brilliant and cultivated man like many of his brothers in the Order. He could or would not sing in the Indian fashion, but recited chants from the liturgy, standing in a cold wind that congealed the blood upon his naked body, while the warriors who had captured him, freshly painted and now bedecked in their best finery, feasted on the ground below him and gravely listened. They did not torture him then, but when they had done, they turned him over to the young men who took him down from the scaffold and began the routine of agony that was to continue, in this place and in the Mohawk towns, for nearly six weeks.

By day he was tied on the scaffold, at the whim of every passer-by, though they were too busy with their fishing to spend a great deal of time on him. But when evening came and he had been taken down, the chiefs would pass among the cabins shouting, "Up! Assemble yourselves, O young men, and come to caress our prisoners." Then they would all gather in the largest cabin and till midnight all would take a hand in turn in torturing him: piercing his foot with a heated rod, tearing out a nail — the warriors kept their own thumbnails long for the purpose; they would drive them under the sufferer's nail and pry it up so that they could pull it with their teeth, with which they then crushed the bleeding end of the finger, or they would place it in the bowls of their glowing pipes until the end charred and the bleeding stopped. They tore out most of his hair and beard, which was offensive to them. They burned his fingers — the first joint on one night, on the next the second. They burned his body with red-hot irons; they made him walk between the fires on pointed sticks driven in the ground. When they tired, they tied him on the ground, hands and legs outspread in a St. Andrew's cross, and the children came from their corners on the sleeping pads to drop hot coals on his body, or reopened his wounds by scratching them with thorns.

A little after midnight, as a rule, they would tire of the sport and take him outside and leave him in the cold, tied to a stake, without covering, unable to sleep, hardly at times with strength enough to turn his mind to prayer. Then a Huron captive, seeking to ingratiate himself, informed the Mohawks that Bressani was a man of importance among the French, the equivalent of a chief, which overjoyed them. They decided that he was too great a prize to be kept merely for the entertainment of a fishing camp: he should be taken home and there be burned to death and eaten. So the following day, which was the twenty-ninth of his captivity, the war party set out for the Mohawk Valley.

Wounded, nearly naked, half starved, and again loaded down with packs, Bressani could barely keep up on the four-day march. Whenever he fell behind, men were sent back to flog him forward. On one occasion he fell into a river and was nearly drowned, but no one would help him. Instead they jeered his feeble efforts to save himself, and that night "they did not omit to burn off one of my nails."

The trail led southwest to strike the Mohawk near present Amsterdam; and the party crossed over to the south bank and struck west, crossing the Schoharie on their way, till they came to the first of the three Mohawk towns. This was Osseruenon, on the site of Auriesville, where Jogues had been tortured with his two lay assistants, Coupil and Couture, and was to suffer martyrdom.

Here again Bressani was led through the gauntlet. His hand was split once more, this time between the middle and forefingers. He was beaten so heavily that he fell to the ground, half dead; but that did not stop the blows, which they continued to rain upon his chest and head. They would probably have killed him then and there in their fury had not the chief intervened to order him dragged to the torture scaffold. They brought him to his senses, once he had been bound to his post, by cutting off his left thumb and a joint of the forefinger; and no doubt they would have kept straight on except for the thunderstorm which broke so violently that they were driven to shelter in their houses.

Bressani and the remaining Huron captives were left naked in the rain till evening, when he was taken down and led into a long house. And now for Bressani and his fellow captives began a new rhythm of abuse in which the nights, though shortest of the year, seemed longer and more dreadful than the days. "Oh my God, what nights!" Jogues wrote, and though it added to his agony of heart to see their tortures, it must yet have brought him comfort to have two French companions to turn to in the brief interludes. Bressani was alone, much of the time separated even from the Huron captives. The Mohawks seem to have accepted him as beyond the common run of men, or victims, and they tormented him through these June nights without a moment of rest:

> *They forced me to eat filth; burned the rest of my nails, and some fingers; wrung off my toes, and bored one of them with a firebrand; and I know not what they did not to me once, when I feigned to be in a swoon, in order to seem not to perceive something indecent they were doing.*

Surfeited with tormenting him there, they sent him and his fellow captives to the second village, Andagoron, where he submitted to similar tortures with the added refinement of being hanged by the feet in chains. For six or seven nights they kept at him; they covered him with coals; they threw hot corn mush on his belly and flanks and called in the dogs to eat, so that their teeth gashed him as they fought for the food; and they inflicted other indignities on him, if that is the proper word, which he refused to describe. "In this manner of living I had become so fetid and horrible that everyone drove me away like a piece of carrion; and they approached me for no other purpose than to torment me…"

Yet now and then, even knowing they would be reviled as cowards if they were observed, one Mohawk or another would seize a moment to help him eat. Without such occasional help, in his now fearful predicament, he would have surely died.

> *…I had not the use of my hands, which were abnormally swollen and putrid; I was thus, of course, still further tormented by hunger, which led me to eat Indian corn raw… and made me relish chewing clay, although I could not easily swallow it. I was covered with loathsome vermin and could not get rid of them nor defend myself from them…*

In his wounds maggots grew; they fell from the stubs of his fingers as he walked about the town. He had an enormous abscess in his thigh that because of his mangled hands he was unable to open; when finally a renegade Huron stabbed it with his knife, it discharged so horribly that the inhabitants of the long house were unable to remain in it and left him alone. And now to please their masters, the Huron captives took to abusing him, except for one thirteen-year-old boy whom the Mohawks put to savage torture in retaliation for his faithfulness, and for Bressani this was almost the hardest cross of all to bear. The boy's sufferings wrung his heart, though he himself was now a walking horror, which even the Mohawks, staring at their own handiwork, could hardly find credible. "I could not have believed," he himself wrote, "that a man was so hard to kill."

It had to come to an end, one way or the other; and on the nineteenth of June the Mohawks met in council to decide his fate. In his own mind Bressani never doubted what it would be, but now, for the first time he gave way and asked one of the chiefs if, after so long a time, his end by burning might not be changed to some other form of death. To his utter amazement, they voted to spare his life. He was given to an old woman to replace her grandfather, and she would have treated him well had not her daughters found his appearance too repulsive to be endured, so finally she sent him to Fort Orange where the Dutch generously ransomed him for about a hundred dollars.

What kept him alive? Ordinarily a captive subjected to torture did not last more than a day, a night, and a climactic hour of the next morning when, again upon the scaffold, his life was offered to Areskoui, the god of war for all Iroquoian Indians. The torture followed a crescendo of mounting fury impossible to stay; the tenacity with which life clung to a human frame was unpredictable. Thus in the Huron town of St. Ignace, the powerful Norman Jesuit, Brebeuf, without once flinching or giving audible acknowledgment of the

THE PERILOUS TREK OF FATHER BRESSANI - 1644

frightful burning he passed through, lived but four hours, while his companion, Gabriel Lalemant, small and frail and at times unable to repress his agony, endured equally savage torments for seventeen.

They had been doomed on capture to die by burning, and their execution was carried out in an explosion of orgiastic fury. Neither Bressani nor Isaac Jogues was treated with quite the same murderous violence. They became, rather, subjects on which the Mohawks could indulge their preoccupation with experimental cruelty, a phase of torture in which they were adept. They often showed a quick perception of their victim's emotional response, trying continually to breach his religious faith; and the more steadfast he proved, the more they came to fear and hate it. This was especially true when the sufferer was an Indian convert. So Bressani was made to watch the agony of his faithful thirteen-year-old convert in the same way that the Iroquois would make a female prisoner watch her baby being burned alive upon a spit and then offer it to her to eat. This was a spiritual violation beyond any physical torture, which on later occasions reached an apex when they substituted a cross for the usual torture posts to roast a Christian and, in eating his flesh while he could still watch them, performed a monstrous parody of the Communion.

Several of the northeastern tribes practiced cannibalism on their captured enemies, but none quite to the extent of the Iroquois, for whom it had definitely a religious significance. Once when a plague of caterpillars nearly destroyed their cornfields, they thought it was because they had not eaten enough of their captives to appease Areskoui, and the situation was quickly remedied. Human flesh seems to have been distasteful to many Indians, who yet ate it because it was a custom they dared not violate — presumably because they would have been considered dangerous radicals if they had refrained. But some tribes seem to have definitely relished it, the Mohawks in particular, whose name to the New England tribes meant "men eaters." Bressani wrote, "In a word, they ate the flesh of men with as much appetite as, and with more pleasure than, hunters eat that of a Boar or a Stag."

If he had died under torture, Bressani would certainly have been eaten, for among many Indians it was believed that if one ate the flesh of a brave enemy, his courage would enter one. Bressani had impressed the Mohawks not only with his courage but by an inner force which enabled him to turn his mind from the pain being inflicted on him and which allowed him also to subdue even the first impulse

Father Isaac Jogues
Survived Iroquois tortures similar to
Bressani's but over a shorter period of time.

of resentment against his tormentors, so that on the contrary, like Jogues, he pitied them; and he found that torture became something he feared more in anticipation than when actually undergoing it.

That the Mohawks sensed this force in him and that it made a deep impression on them is borne out in the narrative: "One evening — while they were burning the ring finger of my right hand for the last time — instead of singing, as they commanded me, I intoned the Miserere in so awful a voice that I made them afraid; and all listened to me with attention."

Though he attributed his survival to the intervention of the Holy Virgin, Bressani also sought to understand the traits of Iroquois character that finally opened the way to his release. Their cruelty, he thought, with its climax in cannibalism, came from a deep inner insecurity, yet at the same time they considered themselves a master race, born to subjugate the world. To torture and eat their captured enemies was an affirmation of superiority. Superstition governed almost every impulse, and for that reason they feared and hated Christianity, which, once accepted, denied the very fears by which they lived. But as they came to respect Bressani as a man, more and more of them dared show him kindness, not only in helping him to eat, but even brushing live coals from his body as others scattered them upon it. When in the end they decided to let him live, they were probably as surprised as he.

During his long ordeal he had had a recurrent dream of waking to find himself suddenly, miraculously healed. But it did not happen so; though free to wander among the houses and even beyond the palisade, he remained a walking spectre, and in his mind he carried the spectre, too, of the death he had escaped. In the evenings he could listen to the veeries calling liquidly along the Auries Kill, and at the same time hear the chiefs' voices inside the palisade summoning the young men to another's torture.

But his courage remained. The Dutch put him on a ship for France. In spite of his precarious health, he returned to Canada the following spring and once more started on his journey to the Huron missions, this time reaching his destination. He served there for four more years, escaping the fate of Brebeuf and Lalemant, and twice making the dangerous journey to Quebec.

During the massacres, tortures etc. taking place in Huronia, the few remaining Jesuits collected together the few Hurons that survived. Collecting what few supplies they could escape with, and over the protests of the Jesuits, some 10,000 took refuge on St. Joseph Island (now Christian Island in Georgian Bay off Penetang). Although the island did offer protection from the Iroquois, the St. Joseph refuge was a mistake. The winter of 1649 and 1650 was spent here in misery, destitution and pestilence of the worst kind to ever be recorded of any of the Canadian Indians. Mothers ate their dead children, children did not hesitate to eat their dead fathers, graves were opened to eat the dead — so great was the hunger experienced.

As spring break-up came, the starving refugees attempted to go to the mainland to seek nuts and roots. Many lost their lives in a watery grave by falling through the melting ice; others met their end by being slain or captured by the Iroquois who still commanded the shores.

The priests were prevailed upon by the Hurons to make an exodus for Quebec and safety. They left in the early summer of 1650 with 300 Hurons, all that could be accounted for of this powerful and proud nation of 30,000 that Champlain visited a quarter of a century before.

The exact route taken is not clearly known. It appears that they walked north, through the district of Muskoka and Parry Sound, arriving at Lake Nipissing or the French River, from whence they travelled the familiar Mattawa and Ottawa route.

The story of their retreat to Quebec was told by Father Ragueneau who journeyed with them and who included this in the Relation for 1650 after he reached Quebec.

> *By roads which covered a distance of about three hundred leagues we marched, upon our guard as in an enemy's country, there not being any spot where the Iroquois is not to be feared, and where we did not see traces of his cruelty, or signs of his treachery. On one side we surveyed districts which, not ten years ago, I reckoned to contain eight or ten thousand men. For all that, there remains not one of them. Going on beyond, we coasted along shores but lately reddened with the blood of our Christians. On another side you might have seen the trail, quite recent, of those who had been taken captive. A little farther on, were cut the shells of cabins abandoned to the fury of the enemy — those who had dwelt in them having fled into the forest, and condemned themselves to a life which is but perpetual banishment. The Nipissirmien people, who speak the Algonquin tongue, had quite lately been massacred at their lake — forty leagues*

in circumference which formerly I had seen inhabited in almost the entire length of the coast — but which, now, is nothing but a solitude. One day's journey this side of the lake, we found a fortress, in which the Iroquois had passed the Winter, coming to hunt men; a few leagues thence, we met with still another. All along, we marched over the very steps of our most cruel enemies.

The Iroquois fortress that Ragueneau alluded to was probably located somewhere on the Mattawa River between Lake Talon and the Town of Mattawa. In this same Relation Ragueneau stated that they came across another such fortress some six or seven miles further on.

The assaults made on the Nipissings were made from these winter quarters of occupation — up the Mattawa, across Trout Lake, along the La Vase and no doubt across the flat lands between Trout Lake and Nipissing over the present site of North Bay.

After building these fortresses on the Mattawa River, they set about to provision themselves with sufficient deer, moose, partridge and rabbits, as well as the necessary herbs and roots to ward off scurvy and other malnutritions caused by an all-meat diet. Having done this they prepared for war against the Nipissings. These fortresses were simply bases of operation, for the Iroquois fighting style (as with all tribes of the eastern woodlands) was to attack and kill quickly, preferably from ambush, and then to retreat for several miles, in order to reappear unexpectedly at some other location.

The assaults against the Nipissings were effective, but not, as Ragueneau suggests, sufficiently devastating to destroy everyone. But they did force the Nipissings to flee. The actual location of any particular battle is not clearly known; nor is the extent of the resistance offered by the Nipissings. That there was resistance and flight, however, is certain, and the available evidence would suggest the following narrative.

The first assault probably came in March, when the crusts on the snow provide the best snowshoeing conditions. The few Nipissing who lived around Talon Lake and Trout Lake had fled to the main body of the tribe on Lake Nipissing, and they took a stand along the western end of Trout Lake, Dugas Bay and Brandy Lake. Although the approach to the La Vase portage was heavily defended the Iroquois drove the Nipissing back to the shores of the main lake. There they took refuge in fortifications already prepared for such a contingency. These fortified villages numbered between one and five, and probably

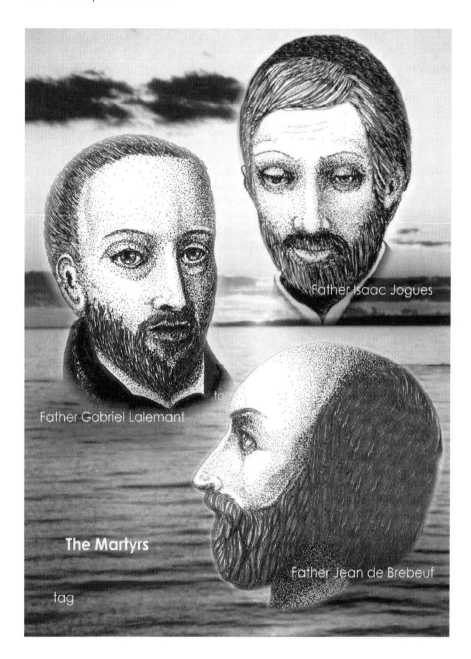

Father Isaac Jogues

Father Gabriel Lalemant

The Martyrs

tag

Father Jean de Brebeuf

These three priests passed through Lake Nipissing on their way to Martyrdom at the hands of the Iroquois. Other priests acknowledged as martyrs include Father Anthony Daniel, Father Charles Garnier and Father Noel Chabanel.

stretched from Callander Bay to Duchesnay Creek, with the main fort located at the mouth of the La Vase River.

The Iroquois also retreated back to their fortifications at Pimissi Bay and the mouth of the Mattawa, dragging their captives with them, to be tortured in the usual fashion. If these captives were not relieved by death during the march itself, then torture at the stake would follow. The Nipissings, of course, were probably dealing with their captives in a like manner, for the Iroquois by no means had a monopoly on platform torture in the eastern woodlands.

A few weeks later, just before break-up, the Nipissings made one desperate raid to drive their enemy from their lands. A few hundred warriors donned war paint, and, carrying as many weapons as they could shoulder, they slipped into snowshoes. They left from Callander Bay, crossed through the woods to Lake Nosbonsing, and after travelling through the woods straight east from Bonfield, swung north to Pimissi Bay for a surprise attack on the Iroquois. A few Iroquois on a hunting foray outside their palisade were quickly silenced, but some escaped to set up the alarm. The main body of the Iroquois party quickly set up an effective defence. The Nipissings made several futile attempts at attacking the fortification. On one charge a number of braves ran in with firebrands in an effort to set the barricade walls afire, but they were shot down by a barrage of enemy arrows and musket fire. The Iroquois had obviously been quick to learn the use of the firearms supplied them by the Dutch.

The Nipissings, having suffered much higher losses than their enemy, and having lost all chance of surprising their foe, soon retreated. Surprisingly the Iroquois did not follow. They were conserving their resources and energies for a future battle, at a time and place of their choosing.

Following the return of the warriors to Lake Nipissing, the Nipissings gathered in council with their chiefs, sub chiefs and elders, for they had a serious decision to make. And they had to take immediate action. It is true that the Nipissings still would not have known the details of the invasion of Huronia or the siege of the French communities, but the very presence of substantial numbers of Iroquois warriors in the midst of their hunting areas was sufficient proof that the Hurons and the French were in serious trouble. The Nipissings could expect no help from that quarter.

In any case what had happened in Huronia was mere speculation.

More important and more immediate was the fact that the Nipissing hunting grounds were occupied by an enemy that they could not drive out. Even if they did not suffer greatly from the actual attacks and tortures of the Iroquois, they would face famine since the whole process of hunting and providing would become a serious and dangerous pursuit with the Iroquois present.

Thus the council decided to flee their home territory. But what course should they take? The country of the Hurons was out of the question. Nor could they risk travelling the French or Ottawa or Mattawa Rivers since it was likely that the Iroquois would have entrenched themselves at the major portages. The only choice was to travel up the Sturgeon River towards the lands of the Cree. It was a logical decision, but nonetheless a most difficult one to make. Most of the men had been on trading expeditions well up the coast of James Bay, but they had never attempted this difficult journey with their families. And now they planned to move the entire tribe! But the decision was made, and all the families were informed. Immediately after Lake Nipissing was sufficiently free of ice, everyone would assemble at the mouth of the Sturgeon River, with whatever bare necessities they could carry in their canoes and across the numerous

IROQUOIS ATTACK ON THE SHORES OF LAKE NIPISSING

portages they would encounter.

On a day late in April of 1650 nearly all the Nipissings beached their canoes along the banks of the Sturgeon River. Some had already moved upstream to the Sturgeon Falls, and a few families from Callander Bay were prevented from setting out because a continual west wind caused the main ice pack to block the mouth of their bay. The wind finally changed, however, and they were able to move out and coast the eastern shore to open water. The delay of those few days would prove disastrous for them.

The La Vase and Mattawa Rivers had been open for a few weeks, Lake Talon for a few days, and Trout Lake had opened up only the day before. Meanwhile the Iroquois had abandoned their winter quarters, and had headed towards Lake Nipissing in search of the Nipissings. The few families from Callander Bay were passing the mouth of the La Vase River just as the Iroquois war canoes came shooting around the last bend of the river. The surprised Nipissings were unable to outpaddle the Iroquois warriors who were not encumbered with families or extra supplies. Their only hope was to head to the sand beach on their starboard side and hope to escape into the woods. But they were too slow, and no sooner had they hit the beach than the Iroquois were upon them. The Nipissing families were killed, scalped and left. Father Ragueneau came across their remains a few weeks later, as he entered the La Vase on his exodus from Huronia.

The Iroquois were set for battle and did not stop at this first encounter to take prisoners. They paddled quickly through the ice-free channel and around the north shore. A few miles to the east of the mouth of the Sturgeon they were spotted by a Nipissing canoe heading for the Sturgeon rendezvous. This canoe quickly gave the warning, and with utmost haste the Nipissing flotilla was launched and headed upstream. The Iroquois war canoes overtook some of the Nipissings, and captured and killed a few more at the first portage. But most of the pursued cleared the portage, and continued north. The Iroquois stopped their pursuit at that point, and returned to deal with their prisoners and any other stragglers that might come along. They remained on the Lake for a few more weeks, during which time they did wipe out the remaining local inhabitants who had not made the main rendezvous. They also had the opportunity to kill the remains of a group of Hurons who passed across Lake Nipissing in their flight from Huronia.

The Nipissings in the meantime continued their flight north, convinced that the Iroquois might be following. They followed the Sturgeon River to the Temagami. Here they encountered their Ojibway cousins who had not encountered any Iroquois, but who were warned that they might. They continued their journey, portaging across to Lady Evelyn Lake and up the Montreal River to the present site of Matachewan. From here they portaged into the tributaries of Nighthawk Lake, and continued down the Frederick House River to the Abitibi. Here they began to encounter encampments of the Cree, their old trading partners. The Cree of course, had heard nothing of the recent Iroquois invasion; in fact few of them had ever seen an Iroquois. The Cree were very sympathetic, but did not encourage the Nipissings to take up residence in their hunting areas. And so on they went, down the Abitibi to the Moose River and out to James Bay.

Again the Cree helped to provide these destitute people with some supplies, mainly geese that had begun to arrive for their nesting season; but they also insisted that the Nipissing not settle on the coast. And so the Nipissings carried on. They coasted James Bay to the mouth of the Albany River. To this point the route was familiar for the

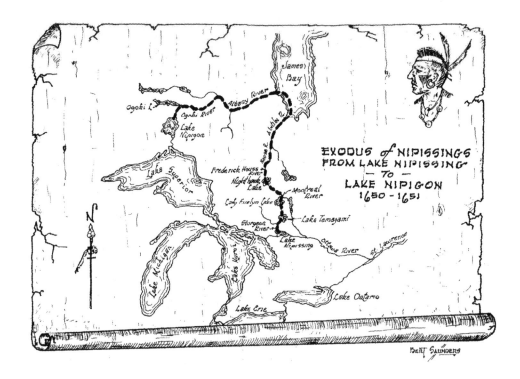

Nipissings had used it for many years in their trade with the Cree.

From this point they did not know what to do. The Crees objected to them joining in their hunting areas. They could go no further north, or they would run into the Eskimo, an ancient enemy of the Indian, that would probably have little difficulty in finishing off this poor and tired band of Nipissings on their own grounds. Besides, the Nipissings knew nothing about living off a salt sea anyway. So they turned west, and went up the Albany River to the Ogaki River and followed it up to Ogaki Lake. A very short portage then placed them in a river system flowing into Lake Nipigon.

The Nipissing had never been to Lake Nipigon before; indeed it is unlikely that they had even heard of it. But it must have seemed like the Promised Land. Here was a large fresh water lake, much like the one they had left. The area was abundant with the type of game they were used to hunting, and their methods of fishing would prove as productive as on Lake Nipissing. Here then the Nipissings made home in time to set up provisions for the coming winter. And here they remained for several years.

Little is known of the area, which includes Huronia, Georgian Bay, and Lake Nipissing in the years immediately following the Iroquois invasions. This vacuum, of course, results from the fact that the only people who recorded events in the 17th century, the Jesuits and French traders, were driven from the region for almost two decades. From traditional histories of Canada the area gets just fleeting mention; and then only to say that the vacuum created in the fur trade by the expulsion of the Hurons was filled by the Ottawas who moved in from the west, and by the French who expanded their operations into the interior. One wonders why the Iroquois did not at least attempt to occupy south central Ontario, after spending so much time and energy in conquering it.

Part of this void was filled by an Ojibway Indian missionary. This was Kah-Ge-Ga-Cah-Bown, the son of an Ojibway chief in the early 19th century. He was educated for a time at a grammar school in Illinois, and eventually was ordained a minister in the Wesleyan Methodist Church in the United States. He is known by his Christian name, Rev. George Copway, and in 1850 he published a book that helps to explain those lost years in Ontario history. It is entitled, *"The Traditional History and Characteristic Sketches of the Ojibway Nation,"* and is particularly valuable since it is based on Indian legends, memories and tribal records. And he tells us that the Iroquois did indeed try to occupy the central portion of Ontario.

> *Before the dispersion of the Hurons no difficulty existed between the Ojibway and the eastern Iroquois, but the western Hurons often waylaid the hunters of the Iroquois nation, and continuing so to do eventually aroused the war-whoop of revenge far and near.*

> *After the year 1608, Champlain traders began to carry on their commercial transactions on the waters of the Mahahmoo Sebee (Ottawa River), which introduced among the Indians fire-arms, woollen goods, and steel for weapons of war.*

> *The next year (1609) Champlain made a treaty with the northern tribes, an examination of which will show in what manner they were to aid them in their wars with the Iroquois. History exhibits the disastrous results following this connection with them.*

> *During a period of thirty-five years the Ojibway on Lake Superior, had been obtaining fire-arms from the French of Quebec. They carried on a peaceful traffic with the French of Lake Superior until the year 1652, when the troubles between the Iroquois and the Ojibway commenced (two years after the Iroquois conquest of Huronia, Nipissing, etc.). The commerce which for thirty-five years had received no interruptions, either from quarrels without or dissensions within, was attacked by the Iroquois, who barbarously plundered and massacred the Ojibway warriors, who had been out for Montreal to barter furs for domestic goods, as also for weapons of war and fire-water. At the entrance of French River, two of this company escaped from the Iroquois, and conveyed an account of the fate of their comrades to the Ojibway at Aunce Bay (Lake Superior). This so incensed the Algonquin tribe that they sent the invaders a message to this effect, that if they ever perpetrated the like again, they would send a few of their warriors in pursuit, to exterminate them. The proud Iroquois laughed in scorn at the threat of the Ojibway, and sent to learn whether the Ojibway included their women in their proposed extermination.*

> *A council of Peace was called by the Ojibway, which was held, according to tradition, below Sault Ste. Marie, at a place called in the Algonquin tongue, Massessauga (mouth of the Mississaga River, near Blind River, Ontario). This council received the deputies of the Iroquois, who concluded a treaty, which they secretly intended not to preserve.*

> *During the summer all lived in peace. They met as friends on the*

shores of the Huron, and as friends hunted in the valley of the Ottawa.

A second offence was committed on the Ojibway, above the Falls, near where Bytown now stands, on the Ottawa River. The Iroquois fell upon a party of the Ojibway, who were hauling their canoes over the carrying place. These they took from them, and also their "fire-water," which they had obtained from the French. About twenty were slain; the remaining swam across the river before their enemies could reach them. Of these, two died on their way home, from hunger and exposure. The rest, three in number, only survived to reach the south shore of Lake Superior, and give information of the attack. The Ojibway were highly exasperated. They were excited to fury, and a desire for revenge reigned in every heart.

The Hurons (exiled Hurons, recently defeated, living with the Lake Superior Ojibway) availed themselves of this favourable opportunity to remind them that they had suffered like cruelties from their brethren. Another council was to be called. The chiefs of the Ojibway were to go to Nahtooway, Sahgeeny [maybe Nottawasaga Bay (Wasaga beach) or mouth of the Saugeen River near Southhampton, Ontario or both], the principal village of the Iroquois, on the easternmost shore of Lake Huron.

They arrived during an Iroquois scalp dance of triumph. It was over the scalps of people of their own nation. For several days they knew not whether they would be massacred or allowed to return; they could get no satisfaction. The sages of the Iroquois knowing however that their people had aggrieved the feelings of the Ojibway, wisely concluded to reflect seriously upon the importance of pressing peace with so powerful a nation as the Ojibway were universally acknowledged to be. They met the Ojibway chief in council, who demanded of them as many packs of furs as warriors they had slain, which the Iroquois chiefs granted amid the manifest dissatisfaction of the people.

The council agreed that the treaty should never be infringed upon, and that it should be held inviolate and permanent. It was a fair, impartial and open treaty, and it was distinctly understood that the first breach of it should be a signal for war between the offenders and the offended.

They scrutinized the features of one another, shook hands, and bade each other farewell.

The chiefs of the Ojibway returned to their own country. Trade was again prosecuted with renewed energy and enterprise, and several valuable loads of furs were sent to the whites of Montreal (known as Ville Marie at this time and until about 1700). No shock of discord was heard; — the shrill war whoop was hushed. Peace dwelt among the mountains of the north.

Without fear the Ojibway and Iroquois hunters met, and spent their evenings together, relating each his adventures and exploits. The Ottawa River was thickly dotted with canoes heavily freighted with furs from the north and west. Blankets were bought with these, and fire-water, which was carried to the extreme end of Lake Superior, and to its northern shores.

The Hurons became so forgetful of their late wars, that they even ventured to accompany the trading Indians (now called Ottawas) down to Montreal, and for one year and a summer they suffered no molestation — all was quiet. The Iroquois saw that the French were more friendly to the Indians of Lake Superior than they were to them; and that the Ojibway were a protection to those by whom they were formerly molested.

The treaty had remained unbroken nearly three years, when bands of the Iroquois waylaid the Ojibway simultaneously at various points on the Mah-ah-moo-sebee (Ottawa River). The news of these unprovoked attacks reached the shores of Lake Superior, but as it was late in the fall, they deemed it imprudent to proceed against the Iroquois, and delayed their expedition until the ensuing spring.

Runners were sent during the winter to the different allies of the Ojibway, the Sacs and Foxes, Menomonies, Kinnestenoes, Pottawatamies, and the Hurons of Sandusky, each of whom were informed of the movements of the great Ojibway family in the west. Strings of wampum were sent from village to village by fleet runners from the extreme end of Lake Superior to the south, far over the prairies of Illinois. The bays of Michigan resounded with the war-cry of the Sacs, while the Menomonies trained their young warriors for the approaching conflict.

The war-dance became a constant exercise, and in fact, the chief amusement of the Indians. The Hurons excited the revengeful feelings of the Ojibway by telling them of the outrages the Iroquois had committed on their children. They shook their war clubs towards the rising sun, and a signal was given that betokened a terrific onslaught.

Their hunting grounds were abandoned, and their women who had attended the cornfields were obliged to fish during the summer, in order to obtain subsistence.

By previous arrangement, the warriors of the nations were to meet below Sault Ste. Marie, at the first changing of the flower moon (May)...

The time arrived. Wah-boo-jeeg's son mustered the war-canoes before the point of Peguahquawom, near the outlet of a deep bay on the south shore of Lake Superior. When the voices of the war-chiefs announced the time of preparation to an eager multitude, a deafening shout arose to heaven, and awoke the echoing spirit of the forest. The rattling of the mysterious Waskeinzke (Deer's Hoof), and the beating of the drum were heard. The tramp of the furious Ojibway and Hurons shook the earth as they danced around the blaze of their council fires.

In the morning, at dawn, the war-canoes from Shahgahwahmik (now La-Pointe) were in sight near Kewaowon (on Lake Superior near Sault Ste. Marie). Two hundred of them approached!

The Sahsahquon (war cry) and song were heard in the distance from over the waters. Never had the waters been agitated by so great a fleet of canoes. The muscular arm of the warriors propelled the canoes with rapid speed on their way.

In former times the old chief, Wah-boo-jeeg, led the warrior bands in person, but being quite aged, he committed the charge to his son, Naiquod. The old chief expressed his approbation of the expedition against the Iroquois, by standing near the edge of a rock which was partially suspended over the waters — from which commanding position he addressed the warriors who were in their canoes ready to go eastward.

I propose in the following chapter to give you the speech of Wah-boo-jeeg, to the assembled warriors, and an account of those battles that terminated in the subjugation of the eastern Iroquois, and of the places at which they were fought.

Copway continues:

In the last chapter we left Wah-boo-jeeg standing upon an overhanging cliff. For a moment he gazed around upon the war-clad throng in canoes before him, then spoke to them as follows:

"When I was young, the Nahtoowassee of the west was heard

from hill to hill. They were as many as the forest trees, but because they had smoked the pipe of peace when their hearts were not right, the Monedoo (a good or kind god) they disobeyed sent our fathers to drive them from our lands, near a lake in the west they called Esahyahmahday (Knife Lake, Minnesota), and they fled west of the father of rivers to dwell in the habitations of strangers. I was the assistant of my father during these bloody wars. — Go, now, at the rising of the sun. The Iroquois have filled the land with blood, and the same Monedoo who was with me on the western plains will be with you to prosper and preserve you."

A shout arose.

"Go," he added, "with your war-clubs — make a straight path to the wigwam of the pale-face, and demand the land of the weeping Huron. I will sit upon the edge of this rock, and await your return."

The old man sat down, and the canoes moved eastward, in search of the foe. The western shore of Michigan was also thronged by the canoes of the Menomonies, Pottawatornies, Sacs and Foxes, — the southern Hurons came with other tribes across the St. Clair (present day Lake St. Clair), and overran the south.

Tradition informs us that seven hundred canoes met at Kewatawahonning (either somewhere on the Manitoulin Island or Tobermory on the Bruce Peninsula), one party of whom was to take the route to Mahamooseebee, (probably Owen Sound-Collingwood shore), the second towards Wahweyagahmah (now Lake Simcoe), and the third was to take the route towards the river St. Clair, and meet the southern Hurons. I will here remark that they had several reasons for waging war against the Iroquois. — First, for having broke the last treaty of peace by the murder of some of their warriors; second, to clear the way of trade between the Ojibway and the French (the Iroquois then lived along the Ottawa River); and third, to regain the land of the western Hurons, and, if possible, drive the Iroquois wholly from the peninsula (meaning all of south, central Ontario).

The warriors who took the Mahamooseebee, had several engagements with them, but outnumbering them, they easily routed the Iroquois. Those who had gone to St. Clair had likewise a fierce battle at the mouth of a river called by the Algonquins, Sahgeeng, and afterwards being joined by the southern Hurons, overran the whole of the south of the peninsula (Bruce Peninsula).

The most bloody battles were fought on Lake Simcoe, at a place called Ramma (actually on Lake Couchiching), at Mud Lake, Pigeon Lake, and Rice Lake: the last that was fought took place at the mouth of the River Trent.

Forty years had nearly elapsed since the Hurons had been routed, but they had not forgotten the land of their birth — the places that were once so dear to them. The thought of regaining their former possessions inspired them with a courage that faced every danger. They fought like tigers. [Copway is wrong here. Actually it was only 10-12 years that had elapsed.]

The first battle between the Ojibway and the eastern Iroquois or Mohawks, was fought at a place near where Orillea [Orillia, Ontario] is now situated, about one quarter of a mile northward. The Mohawks collected in great numbers here, and awaited the attack of the western Hurons and Ojibway. They resisted stoutly for three days — at the close of which, tradition informs us, they sued for mercy, which was granted, and the few survivors were allowed to go to Lake Huron, where they remained during the rest of the war.

The second battle of any account was fought at Pigeon Lake, where the Iroquois had made a strong fort, remains of which are to be seen at this day (1850). At this place great numbers of the Ojibway were killed. For a time the result was doubtful, but finally the Ojibway took the fort by storm, and but few of the Iroquois were spared.

The third battle was fought near Mud Lake, about twelve miles north of Peterboro. Not a male person was spared, and the next day another village that stood on the present site of Peterboro and Smithtown was attacked, and an immense number slaughtered.

I will not attempt to narrate the many barbarous acts that took place on both sides, for humanity shudders at the bare thought of them. They spared none. It is said that they fought the last few who resisted, on a shoal in the river, with arrows, spears, and other missiles; that their blood dyed the water, and their bodies filled the stream.

From both banks of the river the wail of woe and grief arose from the orphan children, whose loud cries and sobs were heard far distant. Here, side-by-side the hostile warriors rolled in blood and agony, while the eagles, buzzards, and crows, flying round and round, added their screech to the noise of the combatants, and by their actions testified their joy that a day of general feasting had arrived.

Slaughter heaped on high its weltering ranks. Death made a throne of the bodies of the slain, and arm in arm with his hand in hand, friend Despair ascended and ruled the day.

The fourth village that they attacked was at the mouth of the Otonabee, on Rice Lake, where several hundreds were slain. The bodies were in two heaps: one of which was slain of the Iroquois, the other of the Ojibway.

Panic-struck the Iroquois collected their remaining forces in Percy, now Lewis' Farm, where for two days and nights they fought like wild beasts. Their shrieks and shouts were heard on each side of the River Trent, so madly did they rush upon destruction.

Of this band of warriors, one alone was saved. The women and children were spared to wander in solitary anguish, and mourn over husbands and fathers whose bones were before them, sad memorials of desolating war. At this day arms of various descriptions are to be found, such as war-clubs, axes, spears, knives, arrow-heads and tomahawks, mixed with human bones.

The fifth and last battle was fought on an island near the mouth of the River Trent, where most of the canoes had collected. At early dawn the warriors landed, and with one wild, fierce rush, commenced their work of havoc and extermination.

Yells and groans were heard on every side, hand to hand they fought, and those who attempted to flee were pursued into the water and there slain and scalped.

When the news of these victories reached the Mohawks, they were incredulous, but soon learned that the Iroquois were entirely broken up and the country subdued.

The war-whoop of the trading Indians and their host abounded. Revelling and feasting celebrated the downfall of the Iroquois. In vain the Iroquois who remained sent to the French, suing for peace. The petitions were not heeded and they vainly attempted to regain by scattered skirmishes a foothold on the land they were destined soon after to abandon forever.

They returned from Canada, and their conquerors allotted them places of habitation. The Shawnees occupied the southern, and the Ottawas and Ojibway the northern parts.

Peace was then restored, and the confines of Niagara and St. Lawrence reaped its benefits.

This took place about 1660, and continued for six years, when the French undertook to lay the foundation of a fort near the foot of Lake Ontario, called in the Algonquin language, Kahtah-nah-queng (i.e. Cataraqui, or Kingston).

Several attempts have since been made by the elder brethren to renew their vengeance against the French, Ottawas, and Ojibway, also to regain their former possessions, but they were unable to succeed, for the whole of the western tribes had combined against them, and they were utterly subdued by overpowering numbers.

Recently the Mohawks, a part of the Six Nations, have settled in Grand River, and others in Bay of Quintee, back of Adolphustown, from the American side, they having been engaged with the British in the wars of that nation...

Although Copway does not specifically mention the Nipissings in his account, they were probably included in the general Ojibway group. We know that by the time of these encounters the Nipissings had returned from Lake Nipigon, and it is unlikely that they would have passed up this opportunity for revenge.

Following this conquest, many of the Lake Superior Ojibway (or Chippewa) made their homes in old Huronia and southern Ontario. Consequently many of the present day reserves in this area are made up of Ojibway Indians. The Iroquois reserves in Ontario (e.g. at Deseronto and Brantford) did not result from these battles, but rather were granted to the American Iroquois by the British government in return for their loyalty to the crown during the American Revolution.

It is interesting to note, I think, that the Copway account receives support from local stories that have been passed orally through the generations. For example, a year ago I was visiting an Ojibway named Alex Knott from the Curve Lake reserve near Peterborough, which was the location of some of the most heavily pitched battles mentioned by Copway. Alex tells a story handed down to him from his grandmother.

Many years ago the Mohawks lived in the Kawartha area — the Ojibway invaded from Georgian Bay and completely wiped out the Mohawk tribe except one boy and one girl. This young couple were left on the shores of Rice Lake. The Ojibway chief said, "We have not completely destroyed your tribe. We leave you two to propagate it once more."

Alex told me that he thought this story had some connection with the famous "Serpent Mounds" of Rice Lake but he was not sure. He did add as well that the Ojibway to this day are not too welcome on the Mohawk Reserves, and that with very little provocation they will turn this story on them, of how their ancestors almost exterminated the Mohawk nation. And after a few drinks, he said, they will bring it up quite forcefully!

tag

Chapter 5

The Re-Discovery and Return of the Nipissings

During their second trip into the interior, 1659-1660, Radisson and Groseilliers wintered with the Chippewa on the south shores of Lake Superior, probably at Chequernegon Bay, the present site of Ashland, Wisconsin. Radisson's diary indicates that a tribe that he was not familiar with visited him on Lake Superior, and that they came from a large lake to the north. This unfamiliar tribe was probably the Nipissings, and they either told Radisson of the country to the north and the east, or introduced him to the Crees. It is even possible that they guided him down the Albany River to the salt water, although I am of the opinion that these two French explorers never actually reached James Bay by land. I do feel, however, that the Nipissings were involved in the knowledge that these two explorers had of the James Bay lowlands and which eventually resulted in the formation of the Hudson's Bay Company. One indication that this is correct is the fact that there were a few Nipissings in the brigade of canoes which Radisson and Groseilliers brought back to the St. Lawrence.

Radisson's dealings with the Nipissing on Lake Nipigon, if there were any, are vague therefore. We can be certain that contact was made with these Indians in their new hunting grounds, however, by Father Claude Allouez. This priest arrived in Quebec in July of 1656, following his training at a Jesuit seminary. In Quebec and Three Rivers he spent six years studying the Huron and Algonquin dialects, and conversing with the work of the nearby Indian missions. In 1664 he was appointed Vicar General of the Northwest, and in August of 1665, he left with a large party of Indians for Chequamagon Bay. This was the site of two large Indian villages, and here would be located the new mission of St. Esprit. The Indians involved were the Huron and Petun refugees from the Iroquois onslaught of 1649-50 and the chapel he built here was the first church erected west of Georgian Bay.

At Chequernagon Bay Allouez first learned of the Nipissings of Lake Nipigon, and on May 6, 1667, he set out to visit them. Travelling in a canoe with two Indians, he crossed the western end of Lake Superior and coasted along its northern shore, reaching the mouth of the Nipigon River on May 25. As they moved slowly up that river, they encountered small hunting parties of Nipissings, and on May 29, Allouez gathered a considerable number of them for Mass, which he celebrated in "a chapel of foliage." The site of this, the first mass celebrated in Canada west of Sault Ste. Marie, can only be guessed at, but there is reason to suppose that it may have been at Virgin Falls, near the head of the Nipigon River.

The following day Allouez set out to visit the village where his little congregation lived. Owing to the spring break-up, it took six days to reach his destination, located somewhere on the southeastern shore of Lake Nipigon. He stayed there two weeks, striving to repair the ravages the intervening years had wrought upon the teachings of Father Pijart. He then returned to Chequernagon Bay.

Because of threats of Sioux attacks, St. Esprit was abandoned in 1671 for St. Ignace, at Michilimackinac, where Father Allouez continued his labours over a vast area comprising much of the present north central United States. He never returned to Lake Nipigon, for by 1671 the Nipissings had returned to their old home on Lake Nipissing. Father Allouez died in 1689 near the present site of Niles, Michigan.

Father Allouez gave the following account of meeting the Nipissings in 1667.

The Nipissiriniens formerly received instruction from our Fathers who sojourned in the country of the Hurons. These poor people, many

tag

of whom were Christians, were compelled by the incursions of the Iroquois to flee for refuge even to Lake Alimibegong (Nipigon), only fifty or sixty leagues from the North Sea.

For nearly twenty years they have neither seen a Pastor nor heard the name of God. I thought that I ought to bestow a part of my labours on that old-time Church, and that a journey undertaken to their country would be attended with Heaven's blessings.

On the sixth day of May of this year 1667, I embarked in a Canoe with two Savages to serve me as guides, throughout this Journey. Meeting on the way two-score Savages from the North Bay, I conveyed to them the first tidings of the faith, for which they thanked me with politeness.

Continuing our journey, on the seventeenth we crossed a portion of our great lake, paddling for twelve hours without dropping the paddle from the hand. God rendered me very sensible aid, for, as there were but three of us in our Canoe, I was obliged to paddle with all my strength, together with the Savages, in order to make the most of the calm, without which we would have been in great danger, utterly spent as we were, with toil and lack of food. Nevertheless, we lay down supper-less at nightfall, and on the morrow contented ourselves with a frugal meal of Indian corn and water; for the wind and rain prevented our Savages from casting their net.

On the nineteenth, invited by the beautiful weather, we covered eighteen leagues, paddling from daybreak until after Sunset, without respite and without landing.

On the twentieth, finding nothing in our nets, we continued our journey, munching some grains of dry corn. On the following day, God refreshed us with two small fishes, which gave us new Life. Heaven's blessings increased on the next day, our Savages catching so many sturgeon that they were obliged to leave part of them at the water's edge.

Coasting along the Northern shore of this great Lake on the twenty-third, we passed from island to island, these being very frequent. There is one, at least twenty leagues long, where are found pieces of copper, which is held by the Frenchmen who have examined it here to be true red copper.

After accomplishing a good part of our journey on the Lake, we left it on the twenty-fifth of this month of May, and consigned ourselves to a River, so full of rapids and falls that even our Savages could go no further: and learning that Lake Alimibogong was still frozen over, they gladly took two days' rest imposed upon them by necessity.

As we drew near our journey's end, we occasionally met Nipissirinien Savages, wandering from their homes to seek a livelihood in the woods. Gathering together a considerable number of them, for the celebration of Whitsuntide, I prepared them by a long instruction for hearing the holy sacrifice of the Mass, which I celebrated in a chapel of foliage. They listened with as much piety and decorum as do our Savages of Quebec in our Chapel at Sillery; and to me it was the sweetest refreshment I had during that Journey, entirely removing all past fatigue.

Here I must relate a remarkable circumstance that occurred not long ago. Two women, mother and daughter, who had always had recourse to God from the times of their instruction, and had received from him unfailing and extraordinary succour, very recently learned by experience that God never forsakes those who put their trust in him. They had been captured by the Iroquois, and had happily escaped from the fires and cruelties of those Barbarians: but had soon afterward fallen a second time into their clutches, and were, consequently, left with no hope of escape. Yet one day, when they found themselves alone with a single Iroquois, who remained behind to guard them while the rest went out to hunt, the girl told her mother that the time had come to rid themselves of this guard, and flee. To this end she asked the Iroquois for a knife to use on a Beaver-skin that she was ordered to dress; and at the same time, imploring God's aid, she plunged it into his bosom. The mother, on her part, arose and struck him on the head with a billet of wood, and they left him for dead. Taking some food, they started forth with all haste, and at length reached their own country in safety.

We spent six days in paddling from Island to Island, seeking some outlet; and finally, after many detours we reached the village of the Nipissiriniens on the third day of June. It is composed of Savages, mostly idolaters, with some Christians of long standing. Among them I found twenty who made public profession of Christianity. I did not lack occupation with both classes during our two weeks sojourn in their country, and I worked as diligently as my health, broken by the fatigues of the journey, allowed. I found more resistance here than anywhere else to infant baptisms; but the more the Devil opposes us, the more must we strive to confound him. He is hardly pleased, I think, to see me make this latest journey, which is nearly five hundred leagues in length, going and coming, including the detours we were obliged to make.

The next that we hear of the Nipissings, they had returned to Lake Nipissing. The story of this encounter was told by Father André who spent three months on that Lake in 1671.

Finding nothing further to live on at the Lake of the Hurons, I was thus by God's will called to that of the Nipissiriniens, to impart my teachings there.

Accordingly, I took a canoe for that lake; and, had I not been with some master canoe men, that night of my departure from Ekaentouton would have been the last of my life. So great was the danger that I have seen nothing like it on the ocean, if I may compare a canoe voyage with that of a ship. During the darkness we passed between rocks that were beaten by the waves with such violence that we seemed every moment about to be engulfed in the waters, even the Savages thinking that we were lost. Yet we were preserved by our Lord's most special mercy, and at length, after many hardships, arrived at Lake Nipissing.

Under the name Outiskouagami, or "long-haired people," are included various Nations of which the principal one dwells in the country of the Nepissirians and on the so-called "Frenchman's River," which connects Lake Huron with Lake Nipissing.

As far as I can judge, the country of these people is very rugged, and little adapted to agriculture; but, in comparison, it abounds in Beavers, nothing but lakes and treeless rocks meeting the eye in nearly every direction.

These rocks were of great service to me, for they are not so sterile as might be imagined, but possess the means of preventing a poor soul from starving. They are covered with a kind of plant, which resembles the scum on marsh that has been dried up by the Sun's heat. Some call it "moss" although it is not at all in the form of moss; others style it "rock tripe"; for myself, I would rather use the name "rock mushrooms". There are two kinds: the small variety is easy to cook, and is much better than the large, which does not cook tender, and is always a little bitter. To make a broth of the first, it is only necessary to boil it; and then, being left near the fire, and occasionally stirred with a stick, it is made to resemble black glue. One must close his eyes on first tasting it, and take care lest his lips stick together.

This manna is perennial, and when one is very hungry he partakes of it without longing for the fleshpots of Egypt. It may be gathered at any season, as it grows on the steep slope of the rocks, where the snow does not lodge so easily as in a flat region.

Extremely abundant here in Summer are blueberries, a small fruit of the size of a pea, and very pleasant to the taste; and besides, before and after the season of snow, there is found in the marshes another fruit, of a red colour and slightly larger. It is sometimes sour, and is liked by those whose teeth are never set on edge.

In some places are oak-trees, but they do not all bear equally good acorns. Once I ate some that were scarcely inferior in taste to chestnuts. Others were bitter, and need to be cooked twelve hours, with occasional changes of water, and to be passed through a sort of lye, in order to be rendered eatable, that is to say, the first boiling is in water containing a good quantity of ashes.

It is not to be wondered at that I am so well posted on the subject of acorns and rock-tripe, as they furnished my chief sustenance during my three months' sojourn here. It is true, I was occasionally given a moose-skin, or even some smoked meat; but that was a feast by no means common. Nature is content with a little, and becomes used to anything. So accustomed did I become to acorns that I ate them almost as one would eat olives, and I was not treated to them so generously as not to leave me very often still hungry for them.

Despite this famine, I did not neglect my duties. I could not entice the Savages to prayers with presents, but my musical instrument came to my aid. I promised them to play on it, and to let them sing my Canticles, after they had prayed. This inducement was so successful that not only did I instruct those who loved the faith, but also those who hated it; for, in their wish to hear their children sing, they learned everything with them, almost without intending to. In the space of three months, they became sufficiently versed in our Mysteries; for it was my unfailing custom, in the morning at daybreak, and in the evening a little before Sunset, to make the round of the Cabins. I explained now our principal Mysteries, now some of my Canticles; again, I questioned the children in their parents' presence, making every one join in public prayers; while finally all would sing together. As a result, my rounds were not, as a rule, completed until very late at night, when nothing was found to eat. Acorns, rock-tripe, and moose-skin were then delicious dishes to me.

These labours gained for me at this mission fourteen Spiritual children by Holy Baptism. If I had felt confidence in the fervour of a number of others, I would have baptized them too; but I believe it is well to try them a little more.

When the ice began to melt I prepared to return to Ekaentouton, where I found occupation for three weeks among the Amikoues, who form the Beaver Nation. There I Baptized nine children, and discharged the same functions as at the other Missions; but I did not find the same scarcity of provisions, for God was satisfied with our previous sufferings from hunger, and gave us the means for ending the winter in comfort, moose being more easily killed at that time of the year.

Missionaries to this country of the Outaoacs must know with St. Paul what it is to experience scarcity much oftener than plenty. Most of our Fathers have, during the past winter, received their share of this grace shown them by our Lord, of suffering something in his service. The souls of these poor Barbarians are precious enough to make us undergo with joy all such hardships; and those who aspire to the happiness of labouring for their conversion must expect to find nothing here, except what nature refuses to have anywhere else.

Father Andre had been sent to the north shore of Lakes Huron and Nipissing to establish missions among these various tribes who were then returning from their long banishment on Lake Superior and environs. In 1675-77 Father Gabrielle Druillette carried on a flying mission throughout the Lake Huron and Nipissing country. Between 1677 and 1680 Father Pierre Baillaquet ministered to the same area. He was succeeded by Father Henry Nouvel for the years 1681-1683. The Relation for 1683 described Nouvel's visit.

Father Henry Nouvel, before going to take charge of the Christians of the Bay des Puans, whither he proceeded a short time ago, made a voyage on Lake Huron on which he navigated more than two hundred Leagues, to visit various petty Algonquin tribes dwelling on the shores of that Lake, to instruct them and to administer to them the Sacraments. He found at Maskounagoung (an Algonkian village on Manitoulin Island), four tribes of Nipissiriniens, and the Achirigouans (an Algonkian tribe), who were celebrating the feast of the dead... They deliver their speeches no longer to the sun, as they formerly did, but to God. They at once erected a bark chapel for the Father, who found them greatly inclined to lead a more Christian life. Drunkenness had almost destroyed them, and had made them completely forget the Instructions that they had received. But they are beginning to have a horror of the evil ways into which it has cast them. Some time ago, they even twice sent back two Canoes loaded with brandy, which the French brought to them; and many have left Nipissing which is their country to avoid occasions in which they do not feel themselves strong enough to resist the excessive tendency that all savages have for drunkenness, and the solicitations of the French, who spare no pains to allure them to it. The Father, after rendering them all the services that they could expect from him, proceeded to Manitoulin.

It is interesting to note that the black robe was not offended by the Nipissings still celebrating the Feast of the Dead, but rather was pleased that they were offering their prayers to God rather than to the sun. This is also the first mention of an extensive liquor flow into the interior. Obviously the fur trade had been fully reorganized after the Huronia disaster of 1649-51, and was beginning to show extensive profits.

tag

Chapter 6

The Nipissings Since 1700

Fort Temiscaming at the lake of the same name was established as a military and fur trading post by the French in the early 1700's. The French listed it in importance with such other forts as Fort Detroit, Fort Niagara, Sault Ste. Marie, Fort Toronto, Fort Frontenac and Michilimacinac. It was located on an island at the mouth of the Montreal River (since flooded out by the dam at Temiscaming, Quebec), and should not be confused with the Fort Temiscaming established in the 1800's by the Hudson's Bay Company near the present town of Ville Marie. This original post was set up to compete with the Hudson's Bay Company, on the Bay itself, to act as a defence from the possibility of an invasion by the English from the north and to act as a staging for French attacks to the Hudson Bay.

It was at this post that the Nipissings traded. In the summer they paddled down the Mattawa and up the Ottawa to Lake Temiskaming. In winter they established a snowshoe trail. They would leave Lake Nipissing, cross to Trout Lake, and climb the hill to Four Mile Lake. From here they would follow the lower lying regions utilizing Anderson, Perchfin and Mitchell Lakes.

At this point after crossing the Jocko River they would change their course from a north easterly direction to east; crossing McConnell Lake, they would start downhill through the Opimika Valley to McLarens Bay on Lake Temiscaming, and on up the ice surface of this lake to the fort. Unfortunately, an Iroquois invasion in 1722 destroyed the fort. It might be of interest to note that Temiskaming was not the most northerly post built by the French. That distinction falls to Fort Abitibi.

Le Moyne d'Iberville and his army, on their cross country trek from New France to the Hudson Bay, for the purpose of capturing the English posts there, stopped at Lake Abitibi to build a duplicate post of Rupert House. The French army used this model to practise their forthcoming attacks. Later, the French continued to use this post as a fur-trading centre.

During the early eighteenth century, a few Nipissings left their homeland and settled near the Jesuit missions of the St. Lawrence. This may not have been so much from religious conviction, as for protection from the Iroquois. These natives were first settled in the Indian mission of St. Louis, near Bout De L'Isle (the upper end of

Montreal Island) under the care of the Sulpicians. About 1706, a fortified trading post was built for them on Isle aux Tortues (an island near the mouth of the Ottawa River) by Vaudreuil, then governor of Montreal, in order to comply with the terms upon which this island had been granted to him in 1702. Upon the removal of the St. Louis mission to the Lake of Two Mountains in 1726 the military operation of Fort Tortues ceased. The Nipissings shared these missions at Lake of Two Mountains with other Algonquin tribes and friendly Iroquois, mainly Mohawk. These Mohawk were ancestors of the people presently living at the Cauwghnawaga Reserve across the St. Lawrence from Montreal and those on the Gibson Reserve south of Bala Ontario. Some of the Nipissings of these missions were assimilated by this Iroquois tribe, and others may have returned to Lake Nipissing after the British set up the Reserve system, or perhaps they spread across other Quebec reserves.

During the French and Canadian campaigns against the British and Iroquois on Lakes Champlain and St. George in the summer of 1757 the French encouraged their allies the Algonquins, Montagnais, Ottawas and Nipissings to join in battle. A Jesuit, whose name has been lost, accompanied these tribes into battle. From the shores of Lake Champlain he gives an account of their actions. The following is that part of his diary dealing with the Nipissings.

> *I met an Abnakis, who, better informed, because he had been braver, told me that this very deadly action had ended with one Nipistingue killed and another wounded in the boarding. I did not wait for the rest of his story; I hastened to rejoin our people, in order to cede my place to Monsieur Mathavot, the Missionary of the Nipistingue Tribe. I was arriving by water when Monsieur de Montcalm who, at the report of the Musketry, had landed a little above, came through the woods; he learned that I had come with news from the place, and applied to me that he might better understand the affair; my Abnakis, whom I recalled, gave him a short report of the combat. The darkness of the night did not permit us to learn the number of the enemy's dead; their barges had been seized and three men had been taken prisoners. The rest were wandering at random in the woods. Monsieur de Montcalm, delighted with these details, retired, that he might, with his accustomed prudence, consider the operations of the next day.*
>
> *The day had hardly begun to dawn when the party from the Nipistingue Tribe proceeded to the funeral ceremony of their brother*

who had been killed on the spot in the action of the preceding night, and had died in the errors of paganism. These obsequies were celebrated with all savage pomp and splendour. The body had been adorned with all the ornaments or, rather, overloaded with all the finery that the most whimsical vanity could use on occasions sad enough in themselves; porcelain necklaces, silver bracelets, ear and nose rings, magnificent garments, everything had been lavished on him; they had borrowed the aid of paint and vermilion in order to make the paleness of death disappear under these brilliant colours, and give the countenance an air of life that it did not possess. None of the decoration of a military Savage had been forgotten; a gorget, tied with a flame-collared ribbon, hung carelessly over his breast; the gun resting on his arm, and the war-club in his girdle; the calumet pipe in the mouth, the lance in the hand; at his side the kettle, filled. In this lifelike and warlike attitude they had seated him on an eminence covered with grass, which served as a bed of state. The Savages, ranged in a circle around the body, maintained for a few moments a gloomy silence, which somewhat resembled grief. The Orator broke this by pronouncing the funeral Oration for the dead; then followed chants and dances, accompanied with the sound of tambourines set around with little bells. In all this appeared an indescribable sadness, sufficiently in accordance with a mournful ceremony. At last, the funeral rites were finished by interring the dead man, with whom they took good care to bury an abundant supply of provisions, fearing doubtless that for want of food he might die a second time. It is not as an eyewitness that I speak; the presence of a Missionary would hardly be in keeping with this sort of ceremony, which is dictated by superstition and adopted by a stupid credulity; I am indebted to the spectators for this account.

It appears that the various Algonquin Allies entered this war with their individual tribal colours. Therefore in a sense a regiment of Nipissings fought under Montcalm in this war. It is not clearly stated anywhere in the Relation, whether these Nipissings were from Lake Nipissing, or the group, previously mentioned, living at the Lake of Two Mountains. I believe they were from both groups. The group at Two Mountains were supposedly fully Christianized. Undoubtedly this dead warrior was not a Christian, nor were his undertakers.

It is also certain that the Nipissings felt a degree of animosity for the English. This was borne out when Alexander Henry the elder ascended the Ottawa River to Mattawa and Lake Nipissing. He was the first Englishman to do so, immediately after the fall of New France to the English, in 1760. His French guide and escort made him dress in French garb and keep his mouth shut while passing through the territory of the Algonquin, Nipissing and Ottawa tribes, for these Indians would forcibly fall upon and slay an Englishman. I'm sure this hatred toward the English was more than verbal patriotism, and was more likely the result of a direct contact with the enemy in past battles.

The Treaty of Paris, 1763, formally ceded Canada to the British, and thus placed all the former native French allies under English rule and control. For a few years the Indians resented and resisted the British, but after the defeat of Pontiac at Fort Detroit, they began to accept the British presence. Accordingly the trade for European goods was resumed.

The Nipissings were to witness white men crossing their territory in greater numbers than ever before, especially after the advent of the North West Company and their large flotillas of voyageur canoes. About 1815, they had their own trading post, Fort Laronde, at the mouth of the La Vase River, the first actual permanent post on Lake Nipissing. After 1821 they also traded at Nipissing House and the Sturgeon River House under the Hudson's Bay Company. These posts are dealt with in greater detail in Chapter nine.

During the 1800s the Nipissing wandered very little from Lake Nipissing. They settled in one place and took on the permanency that they possess today. Colin Rankin, a Hudson's Bay Factor at Mattawa House wrote in his diary in 1849:

> *The Indians in general are not so much against tilling the soil as asserted by some historians. They are said to call farming ignoble and only fit for women and children — all hunting! Look at the Indians of Nipissing. Not one but is more or less engaged in the peaceful and unhunter-like occupation and they are sensible of the advantages they enjoy by their labours. Each one has a little cottage. He has his little garden in the most pleasing condition, not only vegetables of every kind are there, but also various flowers.*

Rankin also notes "a great many Indians belonging to this place (Lake Nipissing) went in July to Lake Huron to receive their annual presents from the government."

The fur traders, however, were not the only people to show an interest in the Nipissing passageway. In the mid-nineteenth century, minerals were found to be plentiful in the Precambrian Shield. To open the lands of the Shield for development it was necessary to purchase, through formal treaties, the lands from the Indians. Accordingly, in 1850 the Government of the Province of Canada sent Benjamin Robinson to perform this task. Treaty No. 61, commonly referred to as the Robinson- Huron Treaty, was the one that concerned the Nipissings. This treaty follows. Our interest should focus on Chief Shabakeshiek, chief of the Nipissings on the north shore of the lake, and Chief Dokis, chief of the Nipissings on the French River.

No. 61

THIS AGREEMENT, made and entered into this ninth day of September, in the year of Our Lord one thousand eight hundred and fifty, at Sault St. Marie, in the Province of Canada, between the Honourable William Benjamin Robinson, of the one part, on behalf of Her Majesty the Queen, and Shinguacouse, Nebenaigoching, Keokouse, Mishequonga, Tagawinini, Shabokeshick, Dokis, Ponekeosh, Windawtegowinini, Shawenakeshick, Namassin, Naoquagabo, Wabakekek, Kitchipossegun by Papasainse, Wagemake, Pamequonaishumg, Chiefs, and John Bell, Paqwutchinini, Mashekyash, Idowekesis, Waquacomik, Ocheek, Metigomin, Watachewana, Minwawapenasse, Shenaoquom, Ouingegun, Panaissy, Papasainse, Ashewasega, Kageshewawetung, Shawonebin and also Chief Maisquaso (also Chiefs Muckata, Mishoquet and Mekis), and Mishoquetto, and Asa Waswanay and Pawiss, Principal Men of the Ojibway Indians inhabiting and claiming the eastern and northern shores of Lake Huron from Penetanguishene to Sault Ste. Marie, and thence to Batchewanaung Bay on the northern shore of Lake Superior, together with the islands in the said lakes opposite to the shores thereof, and inland to the height of land which separates the territory covered by the charter of the Honourable Hudson's Bay Company from Canada, as well as all unconceded lands within the limits of Canada West to which they have any just claim, of the other part, Witnesseth: that for and in consideration of the sum of two thousand pounds of good and lawful money of Upper Canada to them in hand paid, and for the further perpetual annuity of six hundred pounds of like money, the same to be paid and delivered to the said Chiefs and their tribes at a convenient season of each year, of which due notice will be given, at such places as may be appointed for the purpose; they the said Chiefs and Principal Men, on behalf of their respective tribes or bands, do hereby fully, freely and voluntarily surrender, cede, grant and convey unto Her Majesty, Her heirs and successors for ever, all their right, title and interest to and in the whole of the territory above described, save and except the reservations set forth in the schedule hereunto annexed, which reservations shall be held and occupied by the said Chiefs and their tribes in common for their own use and benefit; and should the said Chiefs and their respective tribes at any time desire to dispose of any part of such reservations, or of any mineral or other valuable productions thereon, the same will be sold or leased at their request by the Superintendent General of Indian Affairs for the time being or other officer having authority so to do, for their sole benefit and to the best advantage. And the said William Benjamin Robinson, of the first part, on behalf of Her Majesty and the Government of this Province, hereby promises and agrees to make or cause to be made the payments on beforementioned; and further, to allow the said Chiefs and their tribes the full and free privilege to hunt over the territory now ceded by them, and to fish in the waters thereof, as they have heretofore been in the habit of doing, saving and excepting such portions of the said territory as may from time to time be sold or leased to individuals or companies of individuals and occupied by them with the consent of the Provincial Government. The parties of the second part further promise and agree that they will not sell, lease or otherwise dispose of any portion of their reservations without the consent of the Superintendent General of Indian Affairs, or other officer of like authority, being first had and obtained; nor will they at any time hinder or prevent persons from exploring or searching for minerals or other valuable productions in any part of the territory hereby ceded to Her Majesty as before mentioned. The parties of the second part also agree that in case the Government of this Province should, before the date of this agreement, have sold, or bargained to sell any mining locations or other property on the portions of the territory hereby reserved for their use, then and in that case such sale or promise of sale shall be perfected by the Government, if the parties claiming it shall have fulfilled all the conditions upon which such locations were made, and the amount accruing there from shall be paid to the tribe to whom the reservation belongs. The said William Benjamin Robinson, on behalf of Her Majesty, Who desires to deal liberally and justly with all Her subjects, further promises and agrees that should the territory hereby ceded by the parties of the second part at any future period produce such an amount as well enable the Government of this Province, without incurring loss, to in- crease the annuity hereby secured to them, then and in that case the same shall be augmented from time to time, provided that the amount paid to each individual shall not exceed the sum of one pound Provincial currency in any one year, or such further sum as Her

Majesty may be graciously pleased to order; and provided further that the number of Indians entitled to the benefit of this treaty shall amount to two-thirds of their present number, which is fourteen hundred and twenty-two, to entitle them to claim the full benefit thereof; and should they not at any future period amount to two-thirds of fourteen hundred and twenty-two, then the said annuity shall be diminished in proportion to their actual numbers.

The said William Benjamin Robinson, of the first part, further agrees on the part of Her Majesty and the Government of this Province that in consequence of the Indians inhabiting French River and Lake Nipissing having become parties to this treaty the further sum of one hundred and sixty pounds Provincial currency shall be paid in addition to the two thousand pounds above mentioned.

SCHEDULE of reservations made by the above named subscribing Chiefs and Principal Men:

1st. Pamequonaishcung and his band, a tract of land to commence seven miles from the mouth of the River Maganetawang and extending six miles east and west by three miles north.

2nd. Wagemake and his band, a tract of land to commence at a place called Nehickshegeshing, six miles from east to west by three miles in depth.

3rd. Kitcheposkissegun (by Papasainse), from Point Grondine, westward, six miles inland by two miles in front, so as to include the small Lake Nessinassung (a tract for themselves and their bands).

4th. Wabakekik, three miles front, near Shebawenaning, by five miles inland, for himself and band.

5th. Namassin and Naoquagabo and their bands, a tract of land commencing near La Cloche, at the Hudson's Bay Company's boundary; thence westerly to the mouth of Spanish River; then four miles up the south bank of said river and across to the place of beginning.

6th. Shawmakeshick and his band, a tract of land now occupied by them and contained between two rivers called White Fish River and Wanabitasebe, seven miles inland.

7th. Windawtegowinini and his band, the peninsula east of Serpent River and formed by it, now occupied by them.

8th. Ponekeosh and his band, the land contained between the River Mississaga and the River Penebewabecong, up to the first rapids.

9th. Dokis and his band, three miles square at Wanabeyakoknun, near

Lake Nipissing, and the island near the fall of Okickendawt.

10th. Shabokishick and his band, from their present planting grounds on Lake Nipissing to the Hudson's Bay Company's Post, six miles in depth.

11th. Tagawinini and his band, two miles square at Wanabitibing — a place about forty miles inland, near Lake Nipissing.

12th. Keokonse and his band, four miles from Thessal River eastward by four miles inland.

13th. Mishequanga and his band, two miles on the lake shore, east and west of Ogawaminang, by one mile inland.

14th. For Shinguacouse and his band, a tract of land extending from Maskinonge Bay, inclusive, to Partridge Point, above Garden River, on the front, and inland ten miles throughout the whole distance, and also Squirrel Island.

15th. For Nebenaigoching and his band, a tract of land (extending from Wanabekinegunning west of Gros Cap to the boundary of the lands ceded by the Chiefs of Lake Superior and inland ten miles throughout the whole distance, including Batchewanaung Bay), and also the small island at Sault Ste. Marie used by them as a fishing station.

Signed, sealed and delivered at Sault Ste. Marie, the day and year first above written, in presence of	Shinguakouce, x	(L.S.)
	Nebenaigoching, x	(L.S.)
	Keokonse, x	(L.S.)
Astley P. Cooper,	Mishequonga, x	(L.S.)
	Tagawinini, x	(L.S.)
George Ironside,	Shabokeshuk, x	(L.S.)
	Dokis, x	(L.S.)
T. M. Balfour,	Ponekeosh, x (L.S.)	
	Windawtegowinini, x (L.S.)	
Allan MacDonell,	Shawenakeshick, x	(L.S.)
Geo. Johnston,	Namassin, x	(L.S.)
	Muckata Mishaquet, x (L.S.)	
Louis Cadot,	Mekis, x	(L.S.)
J.B. Assikinock,	Maisquaso, x	(L.S.)
T.W. Keating,	Naoquagabo,	(L.S.)
Jos. Wilson,	Wabokekik, x	(L.S.)
Penetanguishene,	Kitchipossegun,	
16th Sept. 1850.	by Papasainse,	(L.S.)
Witness to the signatures of	Wagemake, x	(L.S.)
Muckata Mishaquet,	Pamequonaisheung, x(L.S.)	

Mekis, Mishoquette,
Asa Waswanay & Pawiss,
T.G. Anderson,
W.B. Hamilton,
W. Simpson,
Alfred A. Thompson.

John Bell, x   (L.S.)
Paqwatchinini, x   (L.S.)
Mashekyash, x   (L.S.)
Idowe-kesis, x (L.S.)
Waquacomiek, x   (L.S.)
Mishoquetto, x   (L.S.)
Asa Waswanay, x   (L.S.)
Pawiss, x   (L.S.)
W. B. Robinson,   (L.S.)
Ocheek, x   (L.S.)
Metigomin, x (L.S.)
Watachewana, x   (L.S.)
Mimewawapenasse, x(L.S.)
Shenaoqum,   (L.S.)
Oningegun, x (L.S.)
Panaissy, x   (L.S.)
Papasainse, x   (L.S.)
Ashewasega, X   (L.S.)
Kagishewawetung \
 by Baboneung, x /   (L.S.)
Shawonebin, x(L.S.)

Reservations continued: —

For Chief Mekis and his band, residing at Wasaquising (Sandy Island), a tract of land at a place on the main shore opposite the island, being the place now occupied by them for residence and cultivation, four miles square.

For Chief Muckata Mishaquet and his band, a tract of land on the east side of the River Naishcouteong, near Pointe aux Barils, three miles square, and also a small tract in Washanwenega Bay, now occupied by a part of the band, three miles square.

Recorded in the office, of the Provincial Registrar, this 22nd day of November, in Lib. "C.M. Miscellaneous," Folio 1, &c.

R. A. TUCKER

Item No. 9 of course describes the Dokis Reserve located on the French River above the Chaudiere Dam, including an island known today as Dokis Island and an area of land on the south shore of the French River between the Restoule and Commanda Creeks. Item No. 10 describes the present familiar Garden Village Reserve. "The planting grounds on Lake Nipissing" is obviously the area of Ernest Couchie's home and taxidermy shop. "To the Hudson's Bay Co. Post" is ambiguous. Does this mean, to the post on the Sturgeon River, and that, since 1850, the present town of Sturgeon Falls and the farmland south, was later carved out of this reserve? Or does it mean to a Hudson's Bay Post, which was located on an island on the north shore of Lake Nipissing, previous to the building of the post on the Sturgeon River, thus defining the western boundary of the present reserve?

During the first half of the nineteenth century, probably because of pressures of increased population, two Montagnais tribes left the Montreal area to live in the wilderness north and south of the Mattawa River. From the research notes of the late Father J.E. Gravelle, parish priest of Chiswick, we learn the following.

Other explorers travelled by our part of the country in later years, but the first letters we can find written about this district in particular, were those of priests sent from Montreal in 1837 to visit the Hudson's Bay Posts at Temiskaming and on Trout Lake, the latter post only fourteen miles from Chisolm. We read this interesting item dated August 11, 1839 preserved in the archives at the Bishop's House, Pembroke: "Authorized by Mgr. I.T. Lartique, Bishop of Montreal, at the Hudson's Bay Post, Trout Lake, a Cross was erected with all possible solemnity, in the presence of my brother priest, Father Hyppolite Moreau, of Ignace Isopantjike and all the men engaged at the Post and a large number of Infidels, assembled to listen to an instruction and to receive the light of the Gospel". SIGNED: H. Moreau and E.E. Piore, Priest. He gives also a list of those then living at Trout Lake, beginning with the telling of the Marriage of Wattagane, major, pagan, chasseur from the Tribe of the Bowl Heads and Marie Otichkwekijikokwe, of the same tribe, privately baptized by an Algonquin at Fort Coulonge and authorized by the Missionaries of the Lake of the Two Mountains to do so. Theirs was the first marriage performed in the Nipissing, and the witnesses were Ignace Isopantjike, Andre Carrier and Joseph Lavale. Two of their children, Paul 6, and Catherine 3, were baptized the same day, along with four other Indian Children: Andre, Marie, Suzanne and Ignace.

Rev. Father Nedelec, stationed many years at Mattawa, and called Father Brulé because he was severely burned by the Indians, who at one time planned to put him to death, left us a precious record concerning the tribes of Indians, who lived in this neighbourhood, just before the coming of the whites about 1859. The first baptism recorded in the Mattawa Parish is that of Henry Timmins, son of Noah Timmins and Henriette Minor, born August 17th, 1859. He and his brother Noah became wealthy miners and gave their name to the town of Timmins.

He tells us that there were four different groups of Indians in this section, each under their own chief and allotted, by agreement, a certain district for their hunting and fishing ground. To the North of the Mattawa River were the Montagnais under Chief Antoine Kikwiwisens. Antoine Creek got its name from him. To the South side of the Mattawa, including Mattawa town, Eau Claire, Rutherglen and on to Chisolm Township were another group of Montagnais under Chief Amable Dufond. Amable Dufond Creek, that flows from Kiosk to Eau Claire, is named after him. The head chief of these two groups lived at the Lake of the Two Mountains, near Montreal. Now we come to our Indians of the Nipissing Tribe, although to be exact, the line of division between them and the last named group of Montagnais would pass North to South, right middle ways through our Township (Chisolm), the boundary being designated as west of Nosbonsing Lake, that is, our Tenth Sideroad. Possibly the waters of Wasi Lake once flooded more land than now, as they did when Booth placed a dam on the outlet, and the Wasi could have been the Southern Part of the boundary. However today we of Chisholm are fortunately all of the same tribe, whether East or West of the Tenth and we share the same hunting ground.

Of the Nipissing Indians, North of Lake Nipissing was Chief Beaucage, after whom Beaucage Bay has been named, and West of Astorville, including at least part of Chisholm, Ferris, North and, South Himsworth and then on, was under Chief Commandant, after whom Lake Commanda had been named. It is thought that this territory extended till it bordered on that of Chief Restoule, farther to the West and South.

Father Gravelle's reference to a Hudson's Bay Post on Trout Lake cannot be substantiated. It is likely that the diary he quotes is referring to the post on Nipissing, or a different Trout Lake. Father Nedelec's nickname "Brulé," so called because his face was burned by Indians, has now been accepted as myth. More probably he received his burns while sleeping alongside a campfire.

Father Gravelle's notes are confirmed from the diary by Colin Rankin of Mattawa House. The following is a passage from that diary.

Sept 27, 1848 – 4 families of Indians arrived from Lake of Two Mountains.

Sept 30 – The Lake Indians left today for their northern hunt.

Oct 25 – Amable du Fond and Simon Couton arrived from Lake of Two Mountains and on their way inland to join their sons.

Dec 13 – The Iroquois passed up to Antoine's camp drawing wood.

Jan 6,1849 – Amable du Fond and Paul arrived in the night.

Feb 6 – Borrowed $10 cash from D. O'Hearn to give the Indians that came yesterday, which they sent to their ladies at Lake of Two Mountains.

At this point in time it appears that these Indians are attending a winter hunt only on the Mattawa, while maintaining their homes at Lake of Two Mountains. Rankin refers to them as Iroquois. Perhaps there were Iroquois with them but for the main part they were Montagnais.

Feb 7 – The Du Fond Indians all started for their land.

April 7 – One of the Nipissing Indians arrived and traded 23 martens. Good eh!

June 10 – Amable du Fond and party arrived on the way down.

Rankin mentions in different parts of his diary the passing of Nipissings by Mattawa House, but unfortunately he does not tell us where they are bound or what their purpose is in travelling.

October 31, 1849 – A family of Indians arrived from Nipissing. This fellow has a pretty little wife, she can give about the most melting and longing glances from her dark peepers. I fear I would not be long proof against such utterly destroying ammunition. I like the childlike confidence that they give a fellow so graciously, with them you are friends in one meeting and should you visit their wigwam, the best is not good enough for you.

November 20 – Young Antoine and Lady arrived intending to hunt not far from the fort.

"Young Antoine" I expect is Antoine Kikwiwisens who was later known as old Antoine, chief of the group of Montagnais north of the Mattawa referred to by Father Gravelle. This is the first mention made of him and I expect 1849 was his first season in his new home. Rankin's diary continues:

November 27 – Du Fond and Lady started up the Du Fond River to hunt. Bastien and Lady also left for their home. About 9 miles below here and 1/2 mile back from the river, there is a small clearing and on this clearing, a small house, a bar, and two small stables. All of these buildings belong to Mr. Bastien and consequently he is the highest up innkeeper. His domicile is generally known by the sobriquet of the "Indian Tavern."

His lady at one time was reckoned terribly handsome — "The belle of the Ottawa." She during her sojourn through life made out to gather together four children. Where they came from no one knows, as she was never married. Bastien fell in with this madam and they were blessed with a fine child, a son. (This Inn was located near the present site of Klock on the CPR east of Mattawa, by far the very first inn in our area. Most travellers on the Ottawa would stop here to refresh themselves.)

> *Dec. 30 – Lady Dufond and her servant arrived to spend New Year's Day with us. She left her lord to take care of the wigwam in her absence. [Rankin is not being facetious in referring to Mrs. Dufond as "Lady." He held the Indians in high esteem, especially the heads of a band, though he could not tolerate drunkenness among them.]*
>
> *Jan. 1, 1856 – Happy New Year… After breakfast the drinking began with a vengeance, old and young, he and she, married and single. Let us leave such a scene – tis sickening almost hellish in appearance. Perhaps you never witnessed the doings of a lot of drinking Indians and squaws.*

It would seem in order to add a few remarks to those of Father Gravelle regarding Father Nedelec. Nedelec was a member of the Oblate priests ministering west of the parish of Mattawa, beginning about 1867. (It would seem that Father Gravelle erred in fixing the date at 1859). Father Nedelec travelled by canoe in summer and snowshoes in winter, as far west as the French River, administering to the spiritual needs of the Montagnais and the Nipissings. As well, he visited shanty men and later held mass along the CPR right of way for the railroad construction crews. He states in his diary that mass was celebrated on Christmas Eve 1882 in a tent constructed by the company at Beaucage. Father Nedelec then was the most recent of the priests to minister in this area, a line that stretched back over two and a half centuries. Yet nowhere have I seen mention of a permanent structure for a church during all those years.

PART 2
The First Europeans

ETIENNE BRÛLE MEETING NIPISSINGS (1610)

Chapter 7

Explorers, Missionaries & Fur Traders

During the French Regime

Étienne Brulé

The first white man to see Lake Nipissing was a French teenager. Étienne Brulé was about 16 years old when he came to Lake Nipissing on a mission for his employer, Samuel de Champlain, in 1610. After Champlain had set up his habitation at the present site of Quebec City in 1609, he engaged four French youths, who would become mapmakers, explorers, and translators of the Indian tongues for his future explorations. Brulé was one of them.

In the spring of 1610, the Hurons and their Algonquin allies arrived on the St. Lawrence where they met Champlain for the first time. They were led by two chiefs, Iroquet and Ochasteguin. Champlain requested that they take Brulé to their country that he might learn their customs and language. They hesitated to take the responsibility, but finally agreed when Champlain accepted the keeping of one of their youths, whom Champlain called Savigon. Champlain then sailed for France with Savigon, and Brulé left for Huronia. A rendezvous was arranged for the following spring on the St. Lawrence.

Thus Brulé became the first white man to ascend the Ottawa. He was the first to cross by way of the turbulent Mattawa, over the height of land called La Vase Portages, and across Lake Nipissing to the French River and then down to Georgian Bay. And he was the first white skin that most of the Nipissings had ever seen. Indeed Brulé travelled a route that would be used by many whites for the next 300 years, till the completion of the CPR. He coasted the Georgian Bay, through the 30,000 islands to Huronia on Matchedash Bay. He spent one year among the Hurons. Brulé had no trouble getting along, and without doubt became one of them. His fine figure and white skin fascinated the Huron maidens, and they sought his embraces. Brulé, with no strong moral training, was not long in taking advantage of the sexual codes of the Hurons. And there is little doubt that within a year of Brulé's first arrival in Huronia the first metis was born in the interior of North America. It is little wonder that a few years later, when the Jesuits came to the Huron country, he would be, on this account, a great hindrance to the spread of Christianity.

Brulé made several trips over this route between Huronia and Quebec. His last trip was probably taken in 1620. In the spring of that year an English raiding party, under the leadership of the Kirke Brothers, captured Quebec and took Champlain prisoner. Probably as bitter to Champlain as the loss of his settlement was the fact that Brulé had turned traitor, in that he had acted as a pilot to guide the British from Tadoussac to Stadacona (Quebec). After Quebec was taken, the English occupants had little use for the traitor and turned on him. Brulé returned to his Indian friends in Huronia. Quebec was returned to France in 1633. In that same year the Indians killed Brulé, and supposedly ate him. There are several theories why. One holds that Brulé had become too depraved even for savage tastes; another contends that he was killed in retaliation for his betrayal of Champlain, the friend of the Hurons.

Father Joseph Le Caron and Samuel de Champlain

After establishing headquarters for New France at Quebec, Champlain sought missionaries to Christianize the Indians of his newly discovered territory. His choice was the Recollet Order, from his hometown of Brouage in France. Father Joseph Le Caron was the Recollet priest that Champlain chose to start missionary work in Huronia.

During a meeting with the Hurons at the St. Louis Rapids on the St. Lawrence in June of 1615, Champlain was pressed by the Indians to fulfill his prior promise of assistance against the Iroquois. Before he could undertake such an expedition, however, he had to return to Quebec for a time to make arrangements for the government of the colony in his absence. He returned to the rendezvous ten days later to find that the Hurons, fearing that he had been taken by the Iroquois, had already departed. With them had gone Father Le Caron and twelve French soldiers. Champlain determined to catch up to them, and on July 9, he set out from the St. Louis rapids with Brulé and ten Indians. Using just two canoes, the party ascended the Ottawa River to the Mattawa. Morris Bishop, one of Champlain's biographers, translated Champlain's diary of this trip into modern geographic terms.

The Ottawa narrowed day by day, amid the grim granite of the Laurentian shield. The travellers portaged endlessly around rapids, where the coppery water leaped white over enormous boulders. Then they would come to long peaceful bights in the lee of evergreen mountains, and would camp on sandy beaches exuding red ochre.

Great fish leaped from the water; vast blue herons laboured heavily into flight. The French fell asleep to the two-toned rattle of the tree toad and the insane laughter of the loon. It was a very disagreeable region, says Champlain, a barren wilderness, uninhabited save for a few primitive fishermen. "It is true that God appears to have been pleased to give his frightful and abandoned region some things in their reason for the refreshment of man and of the inhabitants of these parts; for I can assure you that along the streams there are such a great quantity of blueberries, which is a small fruit very good to eat, and many raspberries and other small fruits, that it is marvellous. The people who live here dry these fruits for their winter supply, as we in France do prunes for Lent."

Thus they came to Mattawa, where the pathway of the Ottawa leads northward. Here, notes Champlain, the eastbound Huron traders may turn north and find their way through an endless series of lakes and little rivers to the system that leads down through Lac St. Jean to the Saguenay and the Tadoussac. The mere thought of such a journey may send a twinge through our civilized muscles.

At Mattawa, Champlain's party left the Ottawa and headed west up the Mattawa River, too violent to permit much paddling. They traversed serene hill-bound lakes: Lake Talon and Trout Lake. From Trout Lake a portage of only three miles took them over the watershed that divides the basin of the Ottawa from that of Lake Huron. From here the streams flow westward, down to the Freshwater Sea.

Bishop states that Champlain made a three-mile portage from Trout Lake to Lake Nipissing, thus indicating the possibility that a trail along the present route of Trout Lake Road and Cassells Street was followed. Nowhere in my research of the area could I find any indication of such a trail. Champlain's own diary entry of this portage reads as follows.

Continuing our way by land, after leaving the river of the Algonquins, we passed through several lakes, where the savages carry their canoes, until, on the twenty-sixth day of the said month, after having made, either by land or by the lakes, twenty-five leagues or thereabouts, we entered the Lake of the Nipissings, in the latitude of 46°15'. This done, we reached the lodges of the savages, where we stayed two days. They gave us a very kind reception and were in goodly number; they are a race who cultivate the soil very little.

During the time I was with them, the chief of these people and others of their head men feasted us on several occasions, according to their custom, and took the trouble to go fishing and hunting in order to entertain us as daintily as they could. These tribes were in number quite seven or eight hundred souls, who live usually on the lake where are a great number of very pretty islands, and among others one more than six leagues long, on which are three. or four fine ponds and a number of beautiful meadows. It is bordered by very fine woods containing plenty of game that haunts these little ponds where the savages catch fish. The north side of the lake is very pleasant; there are fair meadows for pasturing cattle and many little streams discharging into the lake.

At that time they were fishing in a lake, very abundant in many kinds of fish; among others a very good one, which is a foot in length, and also other varieties that the savages catch in order to dry and to lay up in store. This lake is some eight leagues wide and twenty-five long, and into it flows a river which comes from the north-west, up which they go trade the goods which we give them in barter and exchange for their furs, with those who dwell there, who live by the chase and by fishing. It is a country stocked with great numbers of animals, birds and fish.

Having rested two days with the chief of the said Nipissings, we re-embarked in our canoes and entered a river flowing out of this lake, and made some thirty-five leagues along it, and passed several little rapids, some by portaging, others by running them as far as Lake Attigouautan.

"Leaving the river of the Algonquins" refers to the Ottawa River. His journey up the Mattawa is not fully descriptive, but the lakes mentioned are, of course, Talon, Turtle and Trout Lakes. He miscalculated considerably in estimating it to be 25 leagues (i.e. 75 miles) from Mattawa to North Bay. He does not mention at all the method of portages used from Trout Lake to Lake Nipissing, but I believe he used the La Vase portage system. As we shall see later in this chapter, Sagard described the La Vase River in travelling with the Hurons ten years later.

The island in Lake Nipissing described by Champlain must be the largest of the Manitous. Again he is inaccurate in describing it as being 18 miles long. Note also that he makes no mention of this island being taboo to the natives; nor have I seen mention of it in any of the other journals or diaries that I have seen. His estimate of the size of Lake Nipissing is a little exaggerated, but close enough. The river entering from the northwest is the Sturgeon River. The Nipissings travelling up this river to trade with those dwelling there refers to the Cree on James Bay. Of course the river flowing out is the French, and Lake Attigouautan is the Huron word for Lake Huron, specifically Georgian Bay.

Bishop described Champlain's arrival on Lake Nipissing "In the heart of the present city of North Bay".

> *Champlain, looking across the ample surface of the lake, blending into sky, felt that he had at last conquered the barrier of the west.*

> *Here he was cordially greeted by the Nipissing Indians, the Sorcerers, of the Algonquin stock. There were seven or eight hundred of them.*

> *They were a prosperous people, great traders. In midwinter their buyers went west to Sault Ste. Marie to exchange their European trade goods for furs brought by tribes from Lake Superior and Lake Michigan. In the spring a party made a forty-day journey to Hudson Bay for the same purpose. In the autumn they visited the Hurons of Georgian Bay, selling dried fish from Lake Nipissing for a winter's supply of corn. They were too busy to have much time for agriculture.*

> *They were sorcerers, holding intimate converse with the devil. Their ability to cast spells and inflict diseases was notorious among the neighbouring peoples, "But," says Sagard, "apart from their magic spells and communications with demons I found them very kindly and polite."*

> *They were very proud of their country, regarding it as the most beautiful in the world. When a French agent was sent to live with them, they assumed that France was very ugly, since the Frenchman had quitted his country for theirs. And indeed it is a lovely land of water and meadow, as Champlain, usually sparing of admiration, remarks.*

> *After two days of rest and canoe repairing he was again on the move. His boatmen headed southward across the Lake, passing the Manitou Islands, then approaching the southern shore, reddish sand topped by evergreens. They found the granite entrance gates to the French River, the Lake's outlet. Now again they were in the harsh country of impervious, un-wasting stone, where only hardy trees may grow in crevices and hollows. Though to us fresh from our cities, it is a beautiful, pure, everlasting realm, to Champlain it was merely disagreeable. "I did not find in all its length ten acres of arable land,*

but only rocks and a country somewhat hilly."

So down the French River, past falls and rapids as the plane of the Laurentian shield gradually inclines till it meets the level of Lake Huron, and the lake water pries into innumerable gaps in the rumpled shore, and the granite hillocks of the shield becomes capes, and islands, and bare stone humps, and finally reefs, as they step down into the wide water. Here at last was the Freshwater Sea, of which Champlain had first heard in 1603, twelve years before, of which he had dreamed ever since.

He was not the first white man to see Lake Huron. Almost certainly Étienne Brulé came here with the Hurons in 1611; and certainly Father Joseph Le Caron and twelve French improvised soldiers preceded Champlain by only a week.

Near the mouth of the French River Champlain met a party, three hundred strong, of Indians he named the Cheveux Releves, the High Hairs, "because they have their hair elevated and arranged very high and better combed than our couriers, and there is no comparison in spite of the irons and methods these latter have at their disposal. Their bodies were elaborately tattooed; their faces painted, some with a lacy pattern, some with one side green, the other red. They had this singularity, or this coquetry: they wore no breechclouts at all." When good brother Sagard saw them, he tried desperately and vainly to avert his eyes. He notes, however, that the women and girls dealt with the males as offhandedly as with gentlemen properly dressed; male nudity, he was astonished to record, did not entail female immorality.

These Indians were later known as the Ottawas; they were the ancestors of the Chippewa and Potawatomies, and of Pontiac and the Prophet. Their home was apparently on the Manitoulin Island.

The story of what followed — Champlain's visit to Huronia, his participation in the Huron fight against the Iroquois at Lake Oneida in New York State, and his return to Huronia — is a familiar one. During his stay in Huronia in the winter of 1616 he noted that some of the Nipissing tribe wintered there also. Champlain expressed the wish to visit with the Nipissing during the winter and to arrange to accompany them on their 40-day journey to the northern sea. He never did take that long journey, however. Among Champlain's other desires was to discover a passage across the continent to the Pacific Ocean. Indeed he thought he had arrived at the Pacific when he first looked across the open waters of Lake Huron, and was disappointed to discover that the waters were fresh, not salt. Substantial financial support would have been required for Champlain to continue this quest of a passage to the Pacific, and such support was not given to him. As Bishop indicates, however, Champlain had other projects too.

Champlain and Father Joseph turned back, with the intention of visiting a tribe of Nipissing Indians who were wintering in this well-fed country. Champlain had a new project. These were the Indians who made annually a forty-day journey to Hudson Bay to buy furs. Champlain proposed to accompany them to fulfill his purpose balked in 1613. No thought of hardship could diminish his desire to see and know.

But on his way to the Nipissing village he had bad news from Cahiague. The Hurons and Algonquins there were at violent odds.

The Hurons had presented an enemy prisoner to Chief Iroquet of the Algonquins, in the expectations that he would be correctly tortured and eaten. But the Algonquins were a little less ferocious than the Hurons. Iroquet took a liking to his prisoner, sent him hunting, and treated him with fatherly kindness. The Hurons were revolted at such impropriety; they sent an emissary, who killed the prisoner in the presence of the Algonquin headmen. These, outraged, immediately killed the emissary. The Hurons responded by attacking the Algonquin settlement, pillaging and wounding. Then the Hurons imposed reparations, as victorious aggressors do, to the extent of six hundred feet of wampum, fifty wampum belts, a large number of kettles and hatchets, and two females. "This news troubled me greatly, for I pictured to myself the awkward situation that might arise both for them and for us who were in their country." Awkward indeed, this was the sort of thing that might develop into a long racial war. The Algonquins commanded the highway of the Ottawa; they could easily block the fur trade entirely. And, to take the short view, they could regard Champlain and his companions as friends of their enemies and could prevent their return to Quebec.

On his way to Cahiague, Champlain stopped at the Nipissing settlement in the hope of arranging his expedition to the North. He learned, however, Iroquet had just been there to gain support in the threatened conflict with the Hurons. Iroquet had paid the Nipissings well with wampum to abandon their northern journey and to assemble their strength at Cahaigue. "If anyone was sorry it was I; for I had quite expected to see in that year what in many preceding years I had sought for with great solicitude and effort amid much toil and risk of my life". He hoped that the trip was merely postponed; he collected much positive information about the northland and inspected trophies from that country, including Buffalo skins.

Arriving at Cahaigue, he found the situation very tense. At the request of the Indians he assumed the role of judge or arbitrator. His interpreter assembled depositions from both sides. At a council of representative chiefs, Champlain took the floor. He urged peace, pointing out the dangers of division when the common enemy, the Iroquois, were aroused. He dealt on the benefits of the fur trade to the Indians, while thinking, as he admits, of the benefits of the fur trade to the French. "Several speeches were made on both sides, and the conclusion was that I should give them my opinion and advice, seeing by their speeches that they referred the whole matter to my decision, as to their father, promising me if I did so that in the future I could dispose of them as seemed good to me, referring the whole settlement to my discretion."

Shortly after the rendezvous of Champlain with Father Le Caron, the priest made preparation to celebrate the first mass to be given in the province of Ontario, on a high promontory overlooking Georgian Bay and near the present village of La Fontaine. The Hurons came from miles around not only to renew acquaintances with Brulé, but also to look with awe at the priest and his rituals, and so many armed soldiers. Champlain, this man of fortitude, chastity, and deep moral convictions, Father Le Caron, the strict and straight-laced Recollet, and Brulé, the immortal scoundrel, formed a reception line to meet the heads of the various Huron clans.

Brulé's activities with the Huron maidens had by this time become legendary, through the local Indian gossip. The young girls had no reason but to assume that all whites were cut of the same cloth. Passing the reception line, they lifted their buckskin, flashed flirting looks with their big sparkling black eyes, and giggled a few selective words in Huron. Crimson showed through the good father's sunburned face. Champlain stammered, "What are they saying, Étienne, what are they saying?" Brulé, rolled doubled up under a cedar sapling, was unable to answer for paroxysms of laughter.

For me to give the impression that promiscuity ran rampant among the Indian tribes, is unfair and untrue. According to Brother Sagard in his writings on the marital status of the Huron and Algonquins (including the Nipissings), "the young people practised sexual activities freely and had a considerable length of time to choose a mate. Once the marriage vows were performed, this was for life. Divorce and infidelity was seldom heard of."

Father Joseph Le Caron and Champlain were taken prisoner in 1629 when Quebec fell to the Kirke brothers. They were taken to England and then sent to France. Canada was returned to France for a sum equivalent to $240,000. Champlain returned to Canada in 1633, and died two years later on Christmas Day, stricken with paralysis at the age of 68. He was a very great man, whose name will ever shine in the honour roll of the builders of Canada. Father Le Caron never returned to Canada; nor did any members of his order, the Recollets.

Jean Nicolet

Nicolet spent about seven years between 1620 and 1629 living with the Nipissings on their lake and journeying with them to their hunting grounds. Nicolet was employed by the Company of New France (the group of one hundred associates) headed by Champlain and Pontgrave. He was stationed on Lake Nipissing for the purpose of maintaining peace with the local Indians, and engaging in the fur trade. Exhaustive research has revealed very little about this particular stage of Nicolet's life. The Jesuit Relations and Champlain's diary inform us simply that during his stay with the Nipissings, he learned their language and customs. He took his place in their council, was highly respected, and occupied his own lodge. Somewhere through the years a full Nicolet diary existed. This has been searched for in vain. It is believed to have been mislaid by the Jesuits, perhaps Father Le Jeune. The Jesuits apparently had the habit of mislaying certain diaries and documents that did not agree with their Relations.

At any rate during such a long stay with the Nipissings, I feel sure that Nicolet must have travelled to James Bay and back with the natives who were accustomed to making this trip frequently. One would have thought that this would have fired Champlain up to the point of mentioning it, but Champlain was having his own problems with the Kirke brothers about the time of Nicolet's return from Nipissing.

Nicolet then, was the first European resident of Nipissing, and he conducted here the first commercial venture in present Ontario. Nicolet was a deeply religious man. Many references are made in the Jesuit Relations, where at the St. Lawrence mission of Sillery, he acted as godfather during the baptism of many Nipissing Indians.

After the return of Canada to France, Nicolet journeyed to Lake

Michigan and the present Green Bay, Wisconsin. So convinced was he, that after crossing the freshwater sea, he would discover China, that he carried Chinese garments for the meeting. Father Charles Garnier says, "He wore a grand robe of China damask, all strewn with flowers and birds of many colours. No sooner did they perceive him than the women and children fled, at the sight of a man who carried thunder in both hands, — for thus they called the two pistols that he held." Indeed, Nicolet had not reached the Chinese, but had discovered the Winnebago tribe of Wisconsin.

His death in 1636 is described as follows.

> *A month or two after his arrival, he made a journey to the three Rivers for the deliverance of a Savage prisoner; which zeal cost him his life, in a shipwreck. He sailed from Quebec, toward seven o'clock in the evening, in the shallop of Monsieur de Savigny, bound for the three Rivers. Before they reached Sillery, a gust of wind from the Northeast, which had raised a horrible storm upon the great river, filled the shallop with water and caused it to sink, after two or three turns in the waves. The passengers did not immediately sink, but clung for some time to the shallop. Monsieur Nicolet had leisure to say to Monsieur de Savigny, "Sir, save yourself; you can swim. I cannot; as for me I depart to God. I commend to you my wife and my daughter." One by one, the waves tore them all from the shallop, which was floating overturned against a rock.*

Nicolet was entombed next to Champlain.

Brother Gabriel Sagard

Brother Sagard was a lay monk of the Recollet order (Franciscan). He spent one year in Huronia, in 1624-1625. During these formative years of the French missions in North America, the Recollets invited the Jesuits to assist them with this task. After the return of Canada to France in 1632, for political reasons, the Jesuits only were allowed to return to the Canadian mission fields.

In an attempt to secure support for the North American missions, Brother Sagard wrote a most fascinating book on his adventures and observations during his year in Canada. This book was published in 1635, and provides a detailed description of his route and observations.

In the following account Sagard was on his return from Huronia; thus he was travelling east from the mouth of the French River to the mouth of the Mattawa River. I have provided the headings to assist the reader in following this trip. "Epiceriny" is one of the several early names for the Nipissing Indians.

French River

Then we went to the mouth of the river, which issues from the lake of the Epicerinys and empties into the Freshwater Sea.

The following day, after having passed a small rapid, we found two small Algonquin lodges erected on the river bank; from them we got a large piece of bark and a small piece of fresh fish in barter for Indian corn. From there, while we thought we were following our route, we found ourselves straying, as we had done the preceding day, in side channels. [He must have been accompanied by Huron boys, for I can't imagine the old Huron warriors getting lost in side channels of the French River.] So we had to load our things and our canoe on our shoulders, and pass through weeds and over a very troublesome hill in order to find the right course; and we had scarcely got back to it when we had to portage everything over six rapids, then again over another long one, at the end of which we found four lodges of Algonquins. They were going on a journey to some very distant districts. We rested a little beside them, then went to make our camp on a little hill near the lake of the Epicerinys, where we were visited by several passing savages.

Lake Nipissing

The following morning, as soon as the sun allowed us to see its light, we embarked on the lake of the Epicerinys, and crossed it in the middle without any difficulty, a stretch of, twelve leagues. It is, however, a little longer because of its slightly oval shape. The lake is very beautiful and delightful to look at, and abounds in fish. What is more remarkable is, if I am not mistaken, that it discharges its waters from two opposite ends, for on the side of the Hurons issues that great river which flows into the Freshwater Sea, and on the side towards Quebec it discharges by a channel seven or eight fathoms wide, but so obstructed with trees blown down into it that one can only pass with great difficulty, continually putting aside the trees with the hand or with the paddles. [La Vase River]

After crossing the lake we encamped on the shore near the channel (leading eastward), a little to one side of a village of the Epicerinys, where were already encamped a number of Hurons who were going to the Saguenay province. We obtained from the Epicerinys a piece of sturgeon in trade for a small clasp-knife which I gave them, for when we tried to give them red glass beads in exchange they took no interest in them, quite unlike other tribes, which make more of the red beads than of other kinds.

La Vase Portages

When morning came we paddled through the channel for about a short quarter of a league; then we landed and walked nearly four full leagues over very vexatious and difficult paths, except two of our men, who to get relief paddled the canoe for some little time along a stream. Nevertheless they found themselves often impeded there and in great difficulties either on account of the shallowness of the water in places or from the fallen trees in it which obstructed their passage. Finally they were compelled to leave the stream and take to the land like ourselves. I carried for my share of the baggage the paddles of the canoe, with another small bundle, and thus loaded I nearly fell into a deep stream while trying to pass over it on long tree trunks that were not very secure; but our Lord kept me safe. And since I was only able to follow our people at a distance, because they were quicker than I on their feet, I often went astray when I was by myself in the thick weeds and among the hills and ravines, in the absence of beaten paths; but by dint of their shouting and calling I would get back to my right direction and join them.

Trout Lake

When this long portage was over we re-embarked on a lake about a league in length, and then after a portage over a fairly small rapid we found a river that runs towards Quebec and embarked on it.

Turtle Lake

From where we left the Freshwater Sea in the Huron country we had steadily worked up-stream as far as the lake of the Epicerinys, and after that we had nothing but rivers and streams, and a current to help us as far as Quebec, although my savages got very little advantage from it.

Pine Lake or Robichaud and Talon Lake

They preferred to take byways over land and through lakes that are very frequent in that district, rather than to follow the direct route.

On the ninth or tenth day after our departure from the Hurons our canoe was so damaged and broken that it let in much water, and my savages were forced to land and encamp near two or three

Algonquin lodges, and to go in search of bark to make another, which they know how to set up and complete in a very short time. While waiting for my men I remained with the Algonquins, who had with them two tame bear-cubs, as big as sheep. These were constantly wrestling, running, and playing together; then it was which should climb quickest to the top of a tree; but when the hour of meals arrived the mischievous animals were always after us to snatch away our bowlfuls of sagamite (Indian corn, ground and boiled into a gruel) with their claws and teeth. Along with their bark my savages brought back a turtle full of eggs, and they cooked it alive under hot ashes with its paws in the air, and made me eat the eggs, which are big and yellow like the yoke of a hen's egg.

This spot was very pretty, sheltered by a very fine grove of big pine-trees very tall and straight and almost all of the same size and height, all pine-trees, without mixture of any other kind of tree, clean and bare of underbrush and thicket, so that it seemed to be the production and work of a first-rate gardener.

Before setting out from that place my savages hung up in it the armorial bearings of our town of Quieunonascaran; for each town or village of the Hurons has its special arms which they set up along the routes as they are journeying, when they wish to be known that they have passed that way. These arms of our town were painted on a piece of birch-bark as large as a sheet of paper; they consisted of a canoe rudely outlined, and in it as many black strokes drawn as were the men themselves, and to indicate that I was in company with them they had roughly depicted a man in the middle above the strokes, and told me that they represented this personage raised so high above the others to show and explain to the passers-by that they had with them a French captain, for so they called me, and at the bottom of the piece of bark they hung a bit of dry wood about half a foot long and three fingers thick, tied by a shred of bark. Then they hung this coat of arms at the top of a pole stuck in the ground, leaning over a little.

Mattawa River

When the whole performance was completed we left in our new canoe, and that day again we portaged over six or seven rapids; but about noon while we were paddling we struck a rock so violently that the canoe was badly injured and it was necessary to sew on a new piece of bark.

I do not here enumerate all the risks we ran and the dangers we encountered on our way, nor all the rapids round which we had to carry all our packs by very long and toilsome paths, nor how many times we risked our lives by drowning in falls and watery gulfs, as happened afterwards to good Father Nicolas and a young French boy, a pupil of ours, who was following him closely in another canoe, because these risks and dangers are so frequent and matters of such daily experience that if I describe them all they would seem hackneyed repetitions. For this reason I am content here to relate some of them, but only when my subject obliges me to do so, and that must be sufficient.

In the evening after long toil we encamped at the top of a rapid, where for a long time I was in doubt as to the source of a great noise, together with a large dark cloud of smoke that I perceived about a league away. I said to myself, either a village is there or the woods are on fire; but I was mistaken in both suppositions, for the great noise and smoke came from a great waterfall twenty-five or thirty feet high between rocky banks, which we came upon next morning [probably Paresseux Falls]. Below this fall, about a harquebus-shot away, we came upon that mighty rock at the water's edge which I mentioned in Chapter 18, as that which my savages believed to have been a mortal man like ourselves and then to have become changed into this stone by permission and will of God. A quarter of a league further we came again to very high land mingled with rocks, flat and level on top, and serving as the boundary and wall of the river. It was here that my people, because they could not persuade me that this mountain had a mortal soul within it to govern and control it, manifested a kind of sullen displeasure towards me, contrary to their usual behaviour. After that we again portaged all our cargo at three or four rapids. At the last of them we made a short halt under shelter of trees during a great storm that had already thoroughly soaked me.

Mouth of the Mattawa

Then again after passing a long rapid where the canoe was partly carried, partly tracked, we went into camp on a point of high land between the river which comes from the Saguenay and leads to Quebec, and that which flows into the interior in the other direction. The Hurons came down to this point to go the Saguenay, and then paddle up-stream. Yet the Saguenay River which enters the great river St. Lawrence at Tadoussac has its course and current quite the reverse way, so these must be two different rivers, and not one single one since they all flow and empty into the same St. Lawrence;

moreover the distance from one place to the other is about two hundred leagues. However I cannot be absolutely certain of anything, because we changed our course so often on our way going and returning from the Hurons to Quebec that it destroyed my feeling of certainty and real acquaintance with the direct route.

Sagard's confusion as to the source of the Ottawa River was very common at that time. He realized that this was a Huron route to Lake St. John and the Saguenay River, but was confused rightly so to the direction of water flow. When the preferable Ottawa route to the St. Lawrence was obstructed by hostile Iroquois, the Hurons and Nipissings did indeed ascend the Ottawa to Lake Temiskaming; on up the Quinze, and upper Ottawa, across dozens of portages, travelling over half the breadth of Quebec until they hit the headwaters of the Saguenay. Little did Sagard know of the complicated geography involved.

We continued our journey and took the right-hand course, for that to the left leads to the Saguenay province; and I must say that the current of the river we have just left, as it enters the other, produces such an effect that we made more that six or seven leagues before I could get it out of my head that we were travelling against the stream, which could not be, and what made me make this mistake was the great difficulty we had in getting around the point, and because all the way along the river as far as the fall, the water rose, swelled, eddied, and boiled up everywhere as if over a fire. Then there were back sets and currents in the water, which kept meeting us for a long time and at such a rate of speed that if we had not been smart in turning out of their way with equal swiftness we might have been lost and sunk in them. I asked my savages whence this could proceed; they replied that it was the devil's doing or the devil himself.

The Jesuits

The self appointed task of the Jesuits was, of course, the Christianisation of the Indians. They chose to perform this task largely from small missions in the interior such as that on the Wye River, Ste. Marie. They are, however, also our chief source of information about the nature of the country and the people in the 17th century.

A typical trip made by the priests up the Ottawa to Lake Nipissing is described by Brother Sagard. The party of canoeists spent two days with the Nipissings and enjoyed fresh food prepared by the natives. He also described the religious beliefs and practices of the Nipissings.

We encamped quite near them and cooked a meal in the Huron manner, but I could not yet eat their sagamite, not on that occasion, being unaccustomed to it, and so I had to lie down without supper, for they had also eaten up on the way a little bag of sea-biscuite which I had taken from the pinnances supposing that it would last me until I reached the Hurons; but found it was so good that they left nothing remaining for the next day. Our bed was the bare earth, with a stone for my pillow, which is more than our men had as they are not accustomed to have their heads higher than their feet. Our house was two pieces of birch-bark laid against four little poles that were stuck into the ground and arranged so as to slope over us. As their practices and their mode of living when they take a journey are almost always the same, I shall now briefly describe how they conduct themselves on such occasions.

In order to practise patience in good earnest and to endure hardships beyond the limit of human strength it is only necessary to make journeys with the savages, and long ones especially, such as we did; because, besides the danger of death on the way, one must make up one's mind to endure and suffer more than could be imagined, from hunger, from the stench that these dirty disagreeable fellows emit almost constantly in their canoes, which is enough to disgust one utterly with such unpleasant companions, from sleeping always on the bare ground in the open country, from walking with great labour in water and bogs and in some places over rocks, and through dark thick woods, from rain on one's back and all the evils that the season and weather can inflict, and from being bitten by a countless swarm of mosquitoes and midges, together with difficulties of language in explaining clearly and showing them one's needs, and having no Christian beside one for communication and consolation in the midst of one's toil. Yet for that matter the savages are quite kind, at least mine were, indeed more so than are many people more civilized and less savage: for when they saw me for several days almost unable to eat their sagamite, so dirtily and badly cooked, they had some compassion for me and encouraged and helped me as well as they could, and what they could was not much. This to me was all to the good, for I had resolved early to endure gladly what God might be pleased to send me, either death or life; wherefore I kept quite cheerful in spite of my great weakness, and often sang hymns for my spiritual comfort and to please my savages, who sometimes asked me to do so, for they do not like to see people sad or peevish, nor yet impatient, because they themselves are far more patient than our Frenchmen commonly are, as I have witnessed on numerable occasions. This gave me much to reflect on, and made me wonder at their firmness and the control they have of their feelings and how well they can bear with one another and support and help one another if need be. And I can truly say that I found more good in them than I had imagined, and that the example of their patience often led me to force myself more resolutely to endure with cheerfulness and courage everything vexatious that happened to me, for the love of God and the edification of my neighbour.

Now when they were in the open country and the hour of encamping arrived, they would seek more fitting spot on the batik of the river for a camp, or in another place where dry wood could easily be found to make a fire; then one of them set himself to look for it and collect it, another to put up the lodge and find a stick on which to hang the kettle at the fire, another to look for two flat stones for crushing the Indian corn over a skin spread on the ground, and afterwards to put it into the kettle and boil it. When it was boiled quite clear it was all served in bowls of birch-bark which this object we carried each one for himself, and also large spoons like small dishes, which are used for eating this broth, sagamite, in the evening and in the morning, the only times in the day when the kettle is boiled, that is to say, after pitching camp in the evening and before starting in the morning. Sometimes also we did without it when we were in a hurry to set out, and sometimes we boiled it before daylight. If two groups used the lodge each one boiled its own kettle, they all ate together, one kettle after the other without any discussion or contention, and every man had his share of both. As for me I satisfied myself with the sagamite as a rule, which pleased me best, although in both there was always dirt and refuse, partly because they used fresh stones everyday, and very dirty ones, to crush the corn. Besides, the bowls could hardly have a pleasant smell, for when they were under the necessity of making water in their canoe they usually used the bowl for the purpose; but on land they used to stoop down in some place apart with a decency and modesty that were anything but savage.

Sometimes they made a meal of Indian corn uncrushed, and though it was always very hard, on account of the difficulty in getting it (thoroughly) cooked, it agreed with me better at first, because I took the grains one by one, and in this way masticated it thoroughly and at my leisure while walking or in the canoe. In places on the river and the lakes where they thought they might catch fish they dragged behind them a line, putting on and fastening to the hook a piece of skin cut from a frog, and sometimes they caught fish with it, which gave a taste to the pot. But when not pressed for time, as on their way down to trade, some of them after having made their evening camp would go and set their nets in the river, in which they often caught good fish, such as pike, sturgeon and carp (not like ours however, neither so good or so big) and several other kinds of fish which we have not got here.

The Indian corn which we ate on our journey they would go and fetch every second day in certain secluded places where on their way down they had hidden it in little bags made of birch-bark; for it would have been too much trouble to be always carrying, each for himself, all the corn needed for their journey. It astonished me greatly how they, could identify so accurately all the places where they had hidden it, without making any mistake, although sometimes it was far away from the trail and in the depth of the woods or buried in the sand.

Their method and contrivance for kindling fire practised by all the tribes of savages are as follows. They take two sticks of willow, pine or some other kind of tree, dry and light, then cut one to about the length of an ell or a little less, and an inch wide or thereabouts, and on the broad edge of it slightly hollow they make a little pit with the point of an knife or a beaver's tooth, and a little notch beside it to carry down upon an end of cotton match, or other stuff quick to take fire the burning powder which was to fall from the hole. They put the point of another stick of the same wood, as thick as your little finger, or a little less, into this hole that has been started, and kneeling on the end of the broaderstick on the ground they twist the other between their hands so quickly and so long that the two pieces of wood are well heated, and the powder that comes away as a result of this movement is converted into fire with which they light one end of their dry cord, and this holds the fire like the match of a harquebus. After that with a few small pieces of dry wood they make a fire to boil the pot. But it must be noted that not every kind of wood is suitable to draw fire from, only the special kind that the savages know how to select. Now when they find difficulty in drawing fire from it, they crumble a little charcoal into the hole or a little powdery dry wood, which they take from some stump. If they have no broad stick, such as I have described, they take two round sticks and tie them together at the two ends, and when they kneel on them they set between them the point of another stick of the same wood, shaped like a weaver's shuttle, and twist it by the other end between their hands as I have described.

To return them to our journey, we only boiled the kettle twice a day, and as I was not able to eat much of it at one time, being as yet unaccustomed to the fare, it may be supposed that I suffered greatly from want, more than my savages who were used to this mode of dining, and besides, smoking quite often during the day deadened their hunger.

The humane conduct of my host was remarkable. Although his only covering was a bear's skin he made me share it when it was raining at night, without my asking; and in the evening he even arranged a place for me to sleep on at night, laying upon it a few small branches and a little reed mat which it is their custom to carry for their own use on long journeys. In compassion for my difficulties and weakness he would not let me row or wield a paddle, and this was no small labour from which to relieve me, in addition to doing me the service of carrying my things and my bundle at the rapids, although he was already well laden with his own goods and with the canoe, which he carried on his own shoulders over the vexatious and painful trails. One day when I took the lead, as I usually did while the savages were unloading the canoe, because although laden they stepped out much more quickly, just as I was getting near a lake I felt the earth shake under me like an island floating on water; indeed I drew back from it very gently and went to a great rock nearby to wait for my companions, for fear of some mishap befalling me. Sometimes also we had to pass through troublesome bogs from which we could only disengage ourselves with great labour; in particular there was a certain marsh beside a lake into which one might easily sink over one's head, as happened to one Frenchman who was so engulfed that if he had not had his legs wide apart he would have been in great danger, and as it was he sank up to his waist.

Sometimes also one has great difficulty in making passage with head and hands through dense woods, in which also a great number of trees that have rotted and fallen on one another are met with, and these one must step over. Then there are rocks and stones and other obstacles which add to the toil of the trail, besides the innumerable mosquitoes which incessantly waged most cruel and vexatious war upon us; if it had not been for my care in protecting my eyes by a piece of thin stuff which I had covering my face, these fierce creatures would have blinded me many times, as I had been warned. It happened so to the others, who lost the use of their eyes for several days, so poisonous is their stinging and biting to those who have not yet become acclimatized. Nevertheless in spite of all pains in protecting myself from them I did not fail to have face, hands, and legs bitten. Among the Hurons, because their country is open and settled, there are not so many mosquitoes, except in the woods and places where there is no wind during the great heat of summer.

We passed through several tribes of savages but we only stayed a night with each, so as to proceed on our way without pause, except among the Epicerinys or Sorcerers, where we halted for two days, both to rest from the fatigue of the journey and to do some trading with that tribe. It was there that I came upon Father Nicolas near the lake, where he was waiting for me. This happy encounter and the sight of each other gave us much joy, and we received mutual comfort, along with some other Frenchmen, during the short time our people stayed there. Our feast consisted of a little fish that we had and boiled pumpkins, which I found more delicious than any food I have ever eaten, so exhausted and worn out was I with hunger. Then we had to set out, each separately with his own company. This tribe of Epicerinys is called Sorcerer because of the great number of these among them, and of these magicians who profess to converse with the devil in little round towers isolated and apart, which they build on purpose to receive oracles in them and to predict or learn something from their master. They are also in the habit of casting spells and inflicting certain diseases that are only cured by one another's special spell and remedy. There are some of those so stricken from whose body serpents issue and long bowels, and sometimes these come out only half way and then re-enter; all which things are devilish inventions of the wicked sorcerers. But apart from their magic spells and communications with the demons I found them very kindly and polite.

It was in this village that inadvertently I lost, to my very great regret, all the notes I had made on the countries, journeys, meetings, and remarkable things we had seen from Dieppe in Normandy up to that point, and I was only made aware of it after meeting two canoes with savages of the Forest tribe.

By 1648 there were from sixty to seventy French among the Hurons and their neighbours; eighteen priests, four lay brothers, workmen who had laid solid foundation stones at Ste. Marie, and a few soldiers. The Jesuits had crossed Lake Nipissing with cattle, pigs and poultry, the former were obviously brought by canoe when they were very young, and a regular farm had been incorporated in Huronia.

Five priests who passed via Nipissing never returned for they entered martyrdom at the hands of the Iroquois. They were Fathers Anthony Daniel, Jean de Brebeuf, Gabriel Lalemant, Charles Garnier, and Noel Chabanel.

After the complete destruction of Huronia the Jesuits remained in Quebec for about 13 years, licking their wounds. In the 1660's the priests again started using the Ottawa, Nipissing route, and travelled far into the interior, to the far corners of Lake Superior, seeking out of refuge their converted Christians who had escaped the onslaught of the Iroquois. And it was there on Lake Nipigon that they had found the Nipissings. The Black Robes continued to use this route until the 1790's. They spread Christianity on the Canadian prairies, throughout the Mid-western states, and down the Mississippi River Valley, where they met their fellow Jesuits coming from New Orleans and spreading their beliefs across the Louisiana territory.

Other French Visitors

Pierre Esprit Radisson was the first true coureur de bois to visit this area. Inasmuch as both he and his brother-in-law, Groseilliers, were Huguenots, they were probably the first Protestants to pass through the Nipissing region.

Groseilliers passed by way of Nipissing in 1654, went south to the future site of Detroit, across the Michigan Peninsula to Lake Michigan, up to Michilimackinac and back to Quebec.

In 1659, Groseilliers and Radisson ascended the Ottawa, dodged the Iroquois as far up as the present city of Ottawa, and found the Ottawa valley to be almost uninhabited by the Algonquins, as they were still taking refuge in the interior of Quebec from the Iroquois. Lake Nipissing was also found to be abandoned. These two explorers continued on to Lake Superior, spent one winter there, probably made contact with the Nipissings on Lake Nipigon, and returned to Quebec the following spring with sixty canoe loads of beaver.

In 1673 Louis Jolliet, a trader accompanied by a Jesuit missionary, Jacques Marquette, used the Nipissing passageway to discover the Mississippi River and descend to within 100 miles of its mouth.

From about 1735-1749, La Verendrye and his four sons crossed Lake Nipissing several times. They were the first white men to abandon their canoes, leave the well known forested area of eastern Canada, and travel across the prairies by horseback and Indian travois. They were the first whites to see the Rocky Mountains.

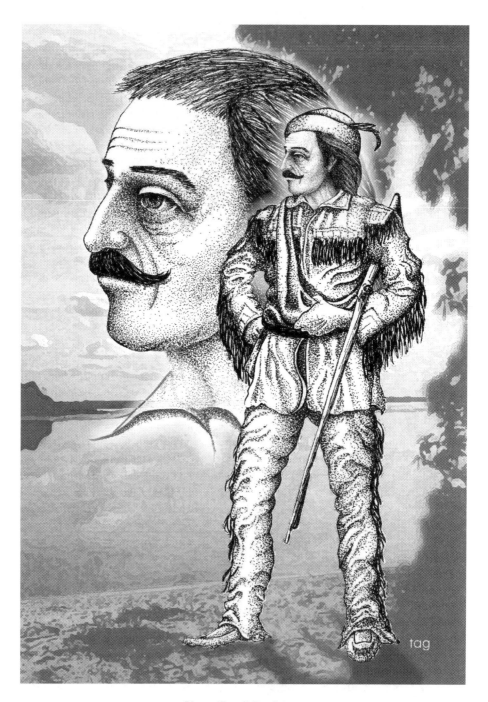

Pierre Esprit Radisson
Inspired by an Arthur Heming woodcut, this illustration shows Radisson on the eastern shore of Lake Nipissing in typical Coureur de bois dress circa 1650.

Pierre Esprit Radisson

They set up fur trading posts with stockades and block houses across the west; Fort St. Pierre on Rainy Lake, Fort St. Charles on Lake of the Woods, Fort Bourbon on the east side of Lake Winnipeg, Fort Dauphin on Lake Manitoba, and Fort Rouge at the junction of the Assiniboine and Red Rivers.

The La Verendryes were the pathfinders, the experimenters. The workability of their system of fur trading was later proven by the British-controlled North West Company that would come 30 or so years later. They were, in fact, the first of the Mountain men that Hollywood has "legendized," Americanized and distorted.

LaVerendrye senior died at Montreal in 1749 on the eve of an approaching departure for the west. His sons tried in vain to obtain leave to take his place. A military leader, Legardeur de St. Pierre, was given this place and profit. He passed via the Mattawa and Nipissing route, and managed to build one more post, Fort Jonquiere at the foot of the Rockies. St. Pierre failed in these ventures.

These were but a few of the French traders and explorers who crossed the Nipissing passageway. Their names have been mentioned here, for they are the more famous of the visitors. But one should not be left with the impression that only a few men in a few canoes passed through Nipissing in this era. Obviously there were several employees, paddlers, and artisans. There were many canoes on these voyages carrying goods to the West and furs to the East. The day of the voyageur had begun. Portages along the Mattawa and French Rivers were taking on French names that are with us today. Lakes and rivers were being named by names that dot modern maps.

The most romantic group of men were the coureur de bois. They were individuals engaged in trapping, fur trading, and on many occasions living with the Indians, returning to civilization only to dispose of their furs and pick up supplies. The voyageur, on the other hand, did not engage in trading or trapping but was simply employed by a fur company to paddle the canoe and portage trade goods into the Canadian interior and to bring furs from the interior. Radisson and Groseilliers would be numbered among this group that, for many years, were looked upon with contempt by French officialdom.

During the granting of seigneuries along the St. Lawrence and lower Ottawa, the Crown insisted that 100% of the labour force apply itself to farming. But the temptations of the fur trade, the chances of gain and adventure, often lured the men of New France to the wilderness. In Frontenac's time 800 men of a total population of 10,000 were absent without leave. King Louis ordered them beaten, branded, and even sent to the galley for life for a second offence. But even the threat of such severe penalties did not stop them.

Although the coureur de bois remain nameless, in the most part, historically, I am sure that several travelled to and from, or lived among the Nipissings. Thus we begin to see the old Algonquin and Nipissing family names changing to French names. A viable new race is created.

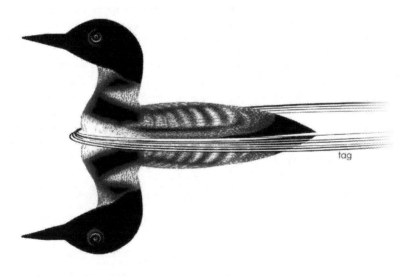

tag

Chapter 8

The Nipissing Passage & the English

Following the Treaty of Paris in 1763, which confirmed that the English would take possession of Canada, the fur trade, centred on the St. Lawrence, also passed from French control. Eager British entrepreneurs quickly established themselves in Montreal and soon were sending their men and supplies into the interior. The newcomers, of course, continued to use the French trading routes, and this meant that Lake Nipissing would continue to be a rendezvous and principal route for the trade.

Alexander Henry (the elder)

Indeed the English began this process immediately after the fall of New France in 1760, three years before the Treaty of 1763. Alexander Henry crossed Lake Nipissing in May of 1761; the first Englishman to do so, His purpose was to assess the prospects of the fur trade in the Canadian interior.

On the Mattawa River he noted: "In the side of a hill on the north side of the river there is a curious cave, concerning which marvellous tales are related by the Voyageurs." This cave is situated on the north side of the river, just below Paresseux Falls. It was called Porte de L'Enfer (gate to Hell) by the early French explorers and voyageurs. The Nipissings and Hurons passed the legend on from one generation to another, and the voyageurs continued the myth and legend that a great spirit in the mortal form of a large animal or monster inhabited the cave.

Daniel Harmon, a clerk with the North West Company, also commented on this cave in May 1800. He wrote, "A large animal remains in it which they call a man eater, and which devours all those who have the presumption to approach the entrance of his solitary dwelling." In 1972, two archaeologists from the University of Toronto, Dr. Alan Tyska and James Burns, along with geologist Dr. Sidney Lumbers, discovered that Porte de L'Enfer was not a natural cave, but an ancient mine worked by Indians for the procurement of red ochre, an ore highly prized by early natives, for decorative purposes.

Alexander Henry continued up to Trout Lake and crossed the La Vase portages:

Alexander Henry,
The first British representative to cross Lake Nipissing was forced to
wear French garb and keep his mouth shut by his (French) guide
for fear of native reprisals toward the English.

On the 26th of August (1761) we reached the portages at la Vase, three in number, and each two miles in length. Their name describes the boggy ground of which they consist. In passing one of them, we saw beaver houses and dams; and by breaking one of the dams, we let off water enough to float our canoes down a small stream, which would not otherwise have been navigable. These carrying-places and the intermediate navigation brought us, at length to the head of a small river that falls into Lake Nipissingue. We had now passed the country, of which the streams now fall north-eastward, into the Outaouais, and entered that from which they flow in a contrary direction, towards Lake Huron... The banks of the little river, by which we descended into the lake, were of an exceedingly delightful appearance, covered with high grass, and affording an extensive prospect.

As the fur trade crept further west, competition between the Montreal traders and the Hudson's Bay Company became fiercer. By mutual agreement between one rival trader and another beginning about 1770, the North West Company was formed in 1779. These partners included merchants, promoters, and explorer-traders. The role of the North West Company in exploring Canada is indicated by the fact that Alexander McKenzie, David Thompson, and Simon Fraser, all famous for the discoveries of the west, across Canada to the Pacific, were all prominent partners.

Alexander McKenzie

McKenzie literally paced, measured, plotted and described his entire route across Canada. His map making and site surveys have been proven by modern instrumentation to be within a very few minutes of latitude and longitude of dead accuracy. McKenzie's journal describes his passage from the mouth of the Mattawa to the mouth of the French River in 1789. Trout Lake was then known as Turtle Lake to the early explorers. They also considered that Lake Nipissing extended down the Upper French to the "Portage Chaudiere" which is the present Chaudiere Dam:

The Petite Riviere [the Mattawa] takes a South West direction, is full of rapids and cataracts to its source, and is not more than fifteen leagues in length, in the course of which are the following interruptions — The portage of Plein Champ [this rapid is now submerged behind a power dam. The name survives in a corrupted

Alexander Mackenzie

*Described and mapped his entire journey across Canada. His maps and site
surveys have proven extremely accurate even by today's standards.*

form in Plain Chant Lake or, lost in English pronunciation, Champlain], three hundred and nineteen paces; the Decharge of the Rose [at the La Rose Rapids], one hundred and forty-five paces; the Decharge of Campion [about half a mile upstream from La Rose Rapids, and probably named after Étienne Campion who accompanied Alexander Henry up the river in 1761], one hundred and eighty-four paces; the Portage of the Grosse Roche [at the Des Roches Rapids], one hundred and fifty paces; the Portage of Paresseux, four hundred and two paces; the Portage of Prairie, two hundred and eighty-seven paces; the Portage à La Cave, one hundred paces [these three portages were all in a one mile stretch of the river, from the Paresseux Falls upstream. Two of them would be around the Paresseux Falls and the Petite Paresseux Falls]; Portage of Talon [at the Talon Chute, near the outlet of Talon Lake], two hundred and seventy-five paces; which for its length is the worst on the communication; Portage Pin de Musique, four hundred and fifty-six paces; next to this is Mauvais de Musique.

These two just-named portages were between Talon Lake, into which the Mattawa broadens above the Talon Chute, and Turtle Lake. A smaller lake further upstream, Lake Robichaud, lies a little to the south, between Talon and Turtle Lakes. On the modern maps Mauvais Musique Rapids are placed on the small river that connects Robichaud Lake and Turtle. This implies that the longer Musique Portage must have been between Lake Talon and Lake Robichaud. It seems clear, however, that the name has been transplanted, and that the fur trade route McKenzie here describes followed the Mattawa between Lake Talon and Turtle Lake. In that event, the Musique and Mauvais portages were around rapids and falls on the Mattawa.

McKenzie continues:

Here is where many men have been crushed to death by the canoes, and others have received irrecoverable injuries. The last in this river is the Turtle Portage, eighty-three paces, on entering the lake of the same name, whence the great river is said to have its source. At the first vase the country has the appearance of having been over-run by fire, and consists in general of huge rocky hills. The distance of this portage which is the height of land, between the waters of the St. Lawrence and the Utawas, is one thousand five hundred and thirteen paces to a small canal in a plain, that is just sufficient to carry the loaded canoe about one mile to the next vase, which is seven hundred and twenty-five paces. It would be twice the distance, but the narrow creek is dammed in the beaver fashion, to float the canoes to this barrier, through which they pass, when the river is sufficient to bear them through a swamp of two miles to the last vase, of one thousand and twenty-four paces in length. Though the river is increased in this part, some care is necessary to avoid rocks and stumps of trees. In about six miles is the Lake Nepisingui, which is computed to be twelve leagues long, though the route of the canoes is something more: it is about fifteen miles wide in the widest part, and bounded with rocks. [Lake Nipissing is fifty miles long and thirty-five miles at its greatest breadth.] Its inhabitants consist of the remainder of a numerous converted tribe, called Nepisinguis of the Algonquin nation. Out of it flows the Riviere des Francois, over rocks of considerable height. In a bay to the East of this, the road leads over the inundates; at the bottom of them are generally found a small number of small stones and pebbles. This circumstance justifies the conclusion, that at some former period these rocks formed the bed of a branch of the portage of the Chaudiere des Francois, [around the first rapid on the French River], five hundred and forty-four paces, to still water. It must have acquired the name Kettle, from a great number of holes in the solid rock of a cylindrical form, and not unlike that culinary utensil. They are observable in many parts along strong bodies of water, and where, at certain seasons, and distinct periods, it is well known the water discharge of this lake, although some of them are upwards of ten feet above the present level of the water at its greatest height. They are, indeed, to be seen along every great river throughout this wide extended country. The French River is very irregular, both as to its breadth and form, and is so interspersed with islands, that in the whole course of it the banks are seldom visible. Of its various channels that which is generally followed by the canoes is obstructed by the following portages, viz. des Pins, fifty-two paces [Now called the Little Pine and Big Pine Rapids, they are the first of a series of rapids extending five miles and ending with the Crooked Rapid]; Faucille, thirty-six paces [the Faucille or Grande Faucille Rapids are now called the Double Rapids and the twist in the river at this point resembles a sickle or "faucille" in shape]; Parisienne, one hundred paces; Recollet, forty-five paces; and the Petite Feausille, twenty-five paces [The Petite Faucille Rapid is on the centre of three channels at the western outlet of the French River. Along this channel canoes could travel westward a dozen miles sheltered by islands]. In several parts there are guts or channels, where the water flows with great velocity, which are not more than twice the breadth of a canoe. The distance to Lake Huron is estimated at twenty-five leagues, which this river enters in the latitude 45.53 North [now given as 45   56' North], that is, at the point of land three or four miles within the lake. There is hardly a foot of soil to be seen from one end of the French River to the other, its banks consisting of hills of entire rock. The coast of the lake is the same, but lower, backed at some distance by high lands.

The Voyageur

With the advent of the North West Company, the Nipissing route was no longer just an explorers' path but became instead the highway that would transport 50% to 75% of Canada's trade. The La Vase portages were no longer indistinct trails but were packed roadways. There are places on this trail where today one can still detect a trench in the soft earth gouged three to four feet deep by the jackboots and moccasins of the voyageur. The physical evidence of the North West Company in our area was a small post at the mouth of the La Vase River, called Fort Laronde. Details about this post are difficult to piece together. However some records do remain in various manuscripts and local publications, and these, with some speculation permit us to piece the picture of Fort Laronde together. Accordingly, there follows an assessment of the evidence available, as well as a speculative account of life at Fort Laronde in the early years of the 19th century,

The first record of this post is found in a North West Company account book dated June 1, 1814, and listing "Sundries, goods, etc. remaining on Lake Nipissingue with Eustache de La Ronde." As La Ronde's name is not found in the North West Company's ledger of servants' accounts for 1811-1821, he may have been more of an agent for the Company than an employee. Three years later Ross Cox describes him as a "free Trader". On Sept. 2, 1817, when he was on Lake Nipissing en route from Montreal to Fort William, Cox recorded that he had "passed a free trader named La Ronde, on his way to Montreal, in a canoe with fourteen packs of beaver, and nearly as many children," and on the next day, after making the "Grand Traverse," Cox recorded that he "arrived at a snug house belonging to Mr. La Ronde's son at which we breakfasted." I checked into the family name of de La Ronde, and found many brothers and sons active in the fur trade on Nipissing before and after the absorption of the North West Company by the Hudson's Bay Company. Later in the 19th century, they operated out of Penetang and Georgian Bay, and

The Voyageur
*In typical costume (scarf, toque & sash) on the shore of Lake
Nipissing this paddler is seeing off his comrades in their huge
'Montreal' canoe. Heading west, this canoe is full of
supplies. Furs will be their cargo on the return trip.*

into Lake Nipissing as free traders. Hence, another Fort Laronde appears in the picture, located on the Georgian Bay near Parry Sound. It should not be confused with the post under discussion.

Several local historians mention Fort Laronde, but it would seem that all references can be traced back to Dr. John J. Bigsby, a contemporary writer who was an eyewitness of the structure. He was allowed a passage in a North West Company canoe from the mouth of the Ottawa River to Sault Ste. Marie in the spring of 1819. His "Pictures of Travel" described the Vaz, or Mud Portages.

> We embarked on the Vaz River circulating slowly among rushes, reeds, cedars, and hemlocks. After a six miles' pull we entered Lake Nipissing at La Ronde, a post of the North-West Company, a decent, ordinary-looking house, not stockaded, with a potato-ground close to it, among marshes and gneiss mounds… We leave Lake Nipissing by the Portage Chaudiere des Francois.

The "decent ordinary-looking house" noticed by Bigsby was presumably the same one described by Ross Cox as the "snug house belonging to Mr. La Ronde's sons."

Bigsby's book was not published until several years after his travels. Apparently Fort Laronde had been moved in the interim for, in a footnote on page 164 he tells his readers that Fort Laronde is "now removed to an island on the North shore, half way between the Vaz River and the Riviere de Francoise. It is considered to be eight to ten miles out of the canoe route to St. Mary's from Montreal."

This would coincide with the notes of Nicholas Garry of the Hudson's Bay Company who travelled from Montreal to Fort William in the summer of 1821. The entry in his Diary for June 19 recorded that his party reached their encampment named "Vase or Morass." On the next day they continued along Riviere La Vase and he noted in his Diary:

> Lake Nipissing came to our View and a Change from Misery to the greatest Pleasure and Comfort… Here we lost the mosquitoes and bathing in the Lake restored us to Cleanliness and comfort. At 9 we breakfasted and started again. Lake Nipissingue is about 12 Leagues in Length [though the Canoe course is more] and 15 miles broad. At 12, our Course W.S.W., we have made the grand traverse and came to a Point called the Isle aux Croix, so named from having 11 crosses on it, the Tombs of 11 Voyageurs who were drowned. We now ran along the South Bank, low land inky with the Pine Trees. There was a

considerable Deal of Swell and it produced all the feeling of Sea Sickness. At half-past one we landed on a rock to Dinner. At half-past two embarked. Our Course now is between Islands but barren Rocks and uninteresting. The North West [Company] have a Post (sic) on Lake Nipissing, but which we did not visit…"

Bigsby's reference to the North West Company's "La Ronde" on Lake Nipissing clearly gives the impression that it was directly on the route to Fort William, but Garry's account rather implies that the post was off the course of the canoes. Unfortunately, after the coalition of the Hudson's Bay Company and the North West Company in March 1821, we are able to find little information about the post on Lake Nipissing.

Alexander McKenzie, that meticulous mapmaker and recorder, passed the site of this post a few times during the last decade of the eighteenth century and did not mention this post. It is probably safe to assume that it did not yet exist. Therefore, it was built sometime after

Fort Laronde
Artist's interpretation of Eustache Laronde's place at the mouth of the La Vase River on the eastern shore of Lake Nipissing.

1800. The first we hear of it is in 1814; but it must have been established before this, because the North West inventories casually mention goods remaining with Eustache La Ronde. Of course these goods were not necessarily in a building at the mouth of La Vase.

Fort Laronde served as the Nipissing rendezvous for the fur trade out of Montreal after 1800. This trade came under the aegis of that conglomerate organization known as the North West Company. The North Westers formed a well-oiled machine. Large brigades of canoes would leave Montreal in the spring, and travel the historical Ottawa, Mattawa, Nipissing, Georgian Bay, Superior route, part of which Champlain had used 150 years earlier, to Grand Portage, and in later years to Fort William, loaded with trade goods for the Canadian North West. In the meantime, large brigades of canoes loaded with fur would leave the trading posts in the West for Lake Superior. Here each brigade would exchange loads and return to their respective posts.

The freight trains used in the route from Montreal to Superior were large, consisting of thirty-two foot birch bark canoes, weighing six hundred pounds and having a beam of six feet, and propelled by ten to fifteen paddling voyageurs. Each canoe would carry five thousand pounds of trade goods or fur, plus voyageurs, and three to four bourgeois passengers (company officials, missionaries, or paying passengers). These particular canoes were known as the Montreal Canoe, or Canot de Maitres. The canoes used in the western section of this fur trade were known as the North Canoe. These were built twenty-two feet in length to allow the craft easier negotiation of the sharp bends of the rivers in the west.

The cargoes from Montreal for the interior were very complete. They included three types of goods; trade items, food and rum for the voyageurs, and items for making camp and repairing canoes. The following items were those carried by "Canot No. 25," which left La Chine on May 6, 1802. The trade articles included tobacco, a variety of cooking pots and pails, hams, salt, grease, brown sugar, port, white sugar, high wine (brandy), rum and spirits, beef, butter, port wine, Madeire Wine, red wine, tongues, sausage, spices, rice, cheese, raisins, figs, prunes, corn and peas. Further trade items were hats, knives, axes, guns, packets of iron and steel, sacs of lead and balls, and canisters of powder.

The food of the voyageur consisted of eight sacs of biscuits (sea biscuits), two sacs of peas, and two hundred pounds of pork, as well as their rations of rum.

The items of camp making and canoe repairing include axes, tin plates, a sail, a roll of birch bark, cooking pots, rope and eighteen pounds of gum.

The trade goods and furs were bundled into ninety-pound packs. Each voyageur was required to carry two such packs across each portage. The first pack was strung onto the back and carried by means of a tump-line across the forehead. This jerked the head backwards. Another such pack was thrown on top of this, rested in the nape of the neck and forced the head forward again. Thus, the voyageur carried one hundred and eighty pounds across the trail and was required by contract to make three such trips, making his total burden five hundred and forty pounds per portage. The voyageur would half run with this load. Many empty-handed bourgeois commented that he could barely keep up. Fort Laronde was one point of visit for these Montreal to Lake Superior voyageurs. After 1821, when the Hudson's Bay Company took over the North West Company, this route fell into disuse for two reasons. One, the Hudson's Bay Company could more profitably service the prairies from Hudson Bay, and second, after the War of 1812 shipping on the upper Great Lakes was well established and the eastern posts could be more effectively serviced by the lake shipping.

The Ottawa and Mattawa no longer heard the songs of the Voyageur. The stillness was broken only by the cry of the loon or the howl of a lonely timber wolf on the hunts. About 1865 the stillness was again broken by the clang of the axe. The lumbermen entered our panorama of things to come, bent on mowing down the huge pine forests ahead of him. Soon he was followed by farmers clearing land and planting seed to feed these axe wielders and their beasts of burden. Shortly after, the railroads followed.

But let us return to the days of the fur trade, and silently witness a visit at Fort Laronde on a warm weekend in June, sometime between 1805 and 1820.

The thirty-two foot Montreal canoe is pushed clear of the swirling waters of the third vase by the resounding swish of fourteen paddlers working in unison. Jules Latulipe is steersman in the lead canoe. Twenty-two canoes follow, some still making the height of land portage from the Ottawa watershed to the Great Lakes watershed; others have crossed and are following in the quite tortuous waters of the La Vase River.

Jules twists the long-steering paddle to port and then quickly back to starboard as the large lively birch-rind canoe negotiates the meandering route followed by the tranquil La Vase. Fort Laronde is around the next bend; so is Lake Nipissing. Jules is anticipating the boisterous welcome they will receive from Eustache Laronde and his congenial wife, a Nipissing Indian, not to mention the freedom from the ever persistent black fly and mosquito which are blown away by the balmy west winds of Nipissing.

But Jules is even more concerned that his bourgeois passengers travelling in the lead canoe, three Company officials and two priests en route to Grande Portage, would for a few days enjoy a semblance of civilization at Laronde, which they were obviously very accustomed to, and had made very clear to this seasoned voyageur that they missed greatly.

Jules makes a long sweep with the steering paddle, fourteen paddles dig into the water, and the graceful craft slides to the right and comes to an easy stop at the log wharf of Laronde. Eustache and the children are waiting on the wharf with hands outstretched to greet the first canoe. Eustache's wife is busy shooing deer from their small potato patch. Smoke is curling from the huge lofty stone fireplace. The faint odour of beans and venison can be detected from the open door of the post; these have been simmering all day in a large iron pot over the open fireplace, in preparation for the expected bourgeois that would be travelling with this brigade.

Eustache instructs the voyageurs to take the personal packs of the bourgeois to the loft quarters where bunks have been prepared for their comfort by Mrs. Laronde. Eustache and his family have set up temporary sleeping quarters for themselves in the fur storage room, back of the trading counter.

Jules and his crew unload their canoe, and pull it onto the shore to inspect in detail any damage that it may have received on the turbulent trip up the Ottawa and Mattawa. If there is damage, this is the time and place for repairs, for Laronde has been equipped as a canoe repair depot.

Others canoes now arrive. Each canoe is beached, unloaded and likewise inspected. Late in the afternoon the last canoe has arrived, camps have been set up from Laronde to the mouth of the La Vase and around an inviting sand beach on the shores of Nipissing protected by a lovely small island covered with huge white pine. Campfires have been lighted and each is heating a large iron pot containing a mixture of pea meal and fat pork, which is always synonymous with the encampment of the voyageur.

The paddlers are stripped and taking a plunge into the La Vase which is deep enough to allow one to dive in directly off the shore. The children have distributed soap that Mrs. Laronde has made during the past winter from a mixture of beaver fat and wood ash. The appearance of the naked bodies of these men of the North is not offensive to Mrs. Laronde. As yet the white man has not entirely convinced the Indian of the presence of any shame in the exposed human frame. Some of the voyageurs are busy with the two priests setting up an altar of rough poplar poles behind the fort itself where Eustache and his wife will receive Holy Communion the next morning, an opportunity they rarely have in this remote place, but one they always take advantage of when a priest passes their door.

Mr. Laronde serves dinner to the bourgeois, set on a huge pine table, set up in the common room of the post for such occasions. The voyageurs sit cross-legged fashion along the full length of the beach enjoying their bill of fare just ladled from the steaming iron pots swinging over numerous campfires. After dinner the voyageurs will receive triple rations of rum and the bourgeois will entertain themselves with high wines.

This has been a tradition as long as Jules could remember during his long engagement with the North West Company, and it had occurred in this area long before Fort Laronde was built. The La Vase portages cross the height of land; the voyageurs have struggled since leaving Montreal, 400 miles behind, against the steady strong currents of the Ottawa and Mattawa Rivers. From here on the remainder of the trip will be downstream.

Therefore Laronde marked a strategic point for such a celebration. Rum casks are emptied, wine bottles drained, a great gaiety takes place on the shore of Nipissing that night as the bourgeois, voyageurs, priests, and the Larondes join in the paddle songs of the men of the North West; songs such as Allouette, En Rouland Ma Boule, A la Claire Fontaine, and Youpe Youpe sur la Riviere.

Surely the well-fuelled campfires, sending a great shower of sparks several feet in the air with each crack of the burning tamarack, and the din of a well developed party has signalled the arrival of this fur brigade to the small band of Nipissings encamped ten miles away on the North shore.

Indeed it had. The next morning several Nipissing canoes, loaded with fresh pickerel, arrive out of the mist at the mouth of La Vase. The Indian has learned that fresh fish is a valuable trade item with the Nor' Westers, as these freight handlers, in their hasty flight from Montreal to Fort William and back between break-up and freeze-up, had very little time to stop and take the fresh food that this land could abundantly provide. Therefore, a fish fry would be a welcome change from their dry beans and peas.

Jules tapped the ashes out of his last pipe for the day, rolled up in his blanket and lay watching the dying embers of his campfire. He was sorry that this would be his last trip into "pays d'en haut." He had very much enjoyed his life as a voyageur in the employment of the North West Company. But he was sixty and maybe next year he wouldn't be able to keep up his end. Many lives had depended on his uncanny ability to swing the long steering paddle just the right amount with instantaneous timing in shooting the wild white waters of the French, Mattawa and Ottawa, not to mention the skill necessary to determine the conditions when they should cross, or not cross, a wide open stretch of water on Lake Superior.

Jules thought back to where it had all started. He remembered vividly when he was nine years old. His father was ploughing one of the stump-strewn fields with a team of aging oxen at the old homestead on the banks of the St. Lawrence, a few miles downstream from Trois Rivieres. A canoe was beached on the river bank at the foot of the field, and the old man walked down to greet the lone paddler. By the time Jules arrived his father was sitting on a rock, an unlit pipe in his mouth, and large tears rolling down his cheeks. "The beloved Montcalm is dead. Quebec has fallen into the hands of the despised British," was the sad news carried by this lone canoeist. It was of little consolation to this old habitant that the British General was also dead.

That night in church the parish priest told them all to maintain faith, that France would surely come to the rescue of Quebec. Jules recalled after church that his father disagreed with this hope of their parish priest. France had allowed her defences of New France to weaken because of her European involvement and she would certainly not be in a position to take the offensive against the British Garrison when she was not able to hold one of the strongest defensive positions in all of North America, the Quebec Citadel.

Therefore, Jules grew up in a double nation, one that at all costs would adhere to everything French, the other that would cause him to work for and with a British commercial system under a British flag. When Jules was sixteen he left home for the first time and was hired by a Scotsman named MacTavish to travel with a small brigade of canoes onto the North Western prairies to seek trade in the fur business. Jules now shuddered to think of the nerve they had to travel this distance with sixteen-foot canoes and two paddlers. They did not know exactly where they were going, to what degree of friendliness they would find each successive tribe of natives, or where or how they would spend the winter. Nor could they be sure of inducing the Indians to trade with them in preference to the Hudson's Bay Company.

As the years went by, however, they were quite successful. Indeed their success forced the giant, the Hudson's Bay Company, to expand their scope and build posts far inland stretching across the great North West plain. For the previous one hundred years the company had thrived by remaining on the Bay itself, but the keen competition created by the traders from Quebec forced them to expand. The Indians no longer needed to travel to the Bay from as far west as the Rockies.

Many small brigades were formed and operated into the west out of Montreal. As time went on these hard business heads of Scots realized that there would be greater profits in cooperating than in opposition in these endeavours. Therefore, they joined together and created the great North West Company, a company that almost brought the Hudson's Bay Company to its knees, and initiated the action that held back the agricultural development of the Canadian prairie for almost one hundred years.

Jules belonged when this Company was formed, and with his vast knowledge of the route and conditions, he quickly advanced to the honoured position of steersman, in the lead canoe of each annual brigade.

Usually the breakfast fires in a voyageur camp are kindled long before daylight, breakfast is eaten and the canoes launched by the first crack of dawn. But this morning the sun is high over the white pine when we hear the first rustlings of a camp just waking up. For this is the only day of rest these paddlers will take on their dash to Fort William. In fact, more a change of pace than a rest, for the canoes must be repaired and loose packs made more secure. The great iron pots are once again steaming, while their contents of beans and salt pork are simmering to an edible softness. Before breakfast is partaken of, many of the voyageurs have joined Eustache and his wife at the poplar pole altar to attend mass and receive Communion. Eustache's old grey lead dog, Babishe, a part husky, cocks his head to the left and stares at the young priest inquisitively. The husky gives a short whine, and then commences a long drawn out howl in response to the chant of the Mass. This sets the rest of the team into simultaneous howling. Eustache steps away from the primitive altar, walks over to the post, and picks a long rawhide whip off a peg on the rear wall. With an easy flick of his wrist, Eustache snaps the long strands of rawhide. The whip cracks like a report from a 50-calibre musket. The huskies dash to the end of their tether seeking shelter, and allow the religious ceremonies to continue without further interruptions. This proves disconcerting to the young priest. This is his first introduction into the Canadian wilderness, but he will have many occasions in the future to administer his services by dog team, canoe, in tepees, log cabins, and fur trading posts, for he is a Jesuit and shall follow the life of many of his brothers who have gone before him.

The Company officials attend as witnesses but do not partake. They think this procedure is very unpresbyterian but have learned over the years not to interfere in what they consider the idiosyncrasies of the French Canadian, for if unriled he makes an excellent Company servant, and gives a day's labour for a day's pay every time.

After breakfast several men enter the swamp back of the post to gather large gobs of spruce gum in birch bark trays. Others are closely examining the external surface of their canoes for cracks and splits in the birch bark covering, and in places scraping many old patches of hardened spruce gum to expose a possible leak. When the gum gatherers have returned the gum is placed in a metal container, slowly heated over the fire and melted to a bubbling, tarry consistency. Varying amounts of beaver tallow are added to inhibit the gum from becoming too brittle after hardening. This mixture, while still bubbling hot, is poured onto the canoe at the area indicated by the previous inspection. It is then buttered or smoothed out by the flat blade of a knife. When the container cools sufficiently that the mixture will not pour, which happens in a very few minutes, it is then replaced on the fire, re-heated and thus the operation is carried on until the last leak is patched.

Some of the voyageurs are busy unpacking the ninety pound packs of trade goods and re-packing them, drawing the tump-lines tight about their canvas coverings, and double checking their leathery knots, to be sure that they will withstand the rugged handling that they will receive over the numerous portages between here and Lake Superior.

Eustache has taken advantage of this visit to seek the assistance of a few brawny arms to help him replace some of the sill logs that have begun to rot in the post. They will also assist him to mix lime and sand and replace some of the chinking between the pine logs around the building, that has become loosened from the contractions caused by the previous winter frosts.

The evening meal will be a welcome change. The fresh pickerel have been exchanged for fire-water, a method of trading the Nor'Westers, without hesitation, have introduced to the fur trade. Each voyageur has received two pickerel weighing about four pounds each. After evisceration each fish is speared with a green stick and held in the glowing embers of the fire until the skin is burned black. It is then withdrawn, the charred skin pulled away, and after a dash of salt, is eaten with the fingers. Each man smacks his lips over this as he thinks back to the first thirty days, three meals a day, of fat pork and beans. The camp retires immediately after supper.

All is in readiness and they will pull out across Nipissing with the first glimmer of daylight on the horizon.

The next morning Eustache and his family are standing on the wharf shaking hands, bidding farewell, and promising these voyageurs to have more fresh fish on their return to Montreal in the fall. As the last canoe disappears into the mist at the mouth of the La Vase, the steady swish, swish of the paddles, and the refrains of "Allouette" can be heard passing from one canoe to the other as they take their bearings from Jules' lead canoe and pass into the open stretches of Nipissing.

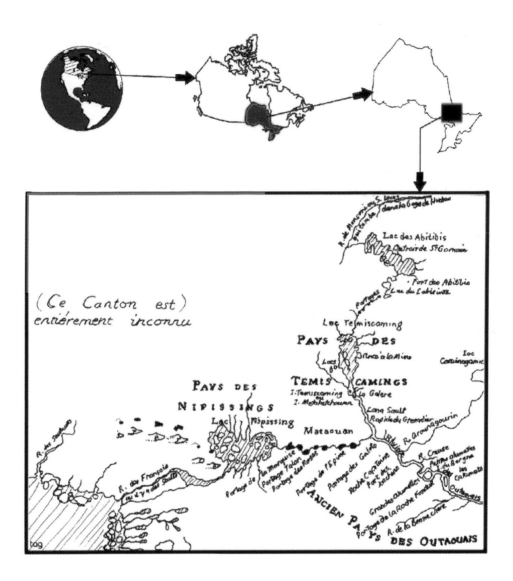

The above map is a recreated detail of the "Carte Des Lacs Du Canada" created by N. Bellin in 1744. This section clearly shows the route and portages from the Ottawa River to Lake Nipissing. Common to most of the early North American maps, it is indicative of the importance this passage had in the early exploration and development of Canada and North America in general.

Ottawa River to Lake Nipissing Voyager Route

The following maps by Bert Saunders detail the Mattawa to Nipissing water route the natives introduced to the early explorers and eventually to the voyageurs who used them to transport trading goods west and furs east as described by Alexander McKenzie. The maps are presented in an east to west format as McKenzie would have encountered them and Bert pays special attention to the portages, most with detailed inserts showing the length of the portages in 'paces'–the equivalent of a man's step.

tag

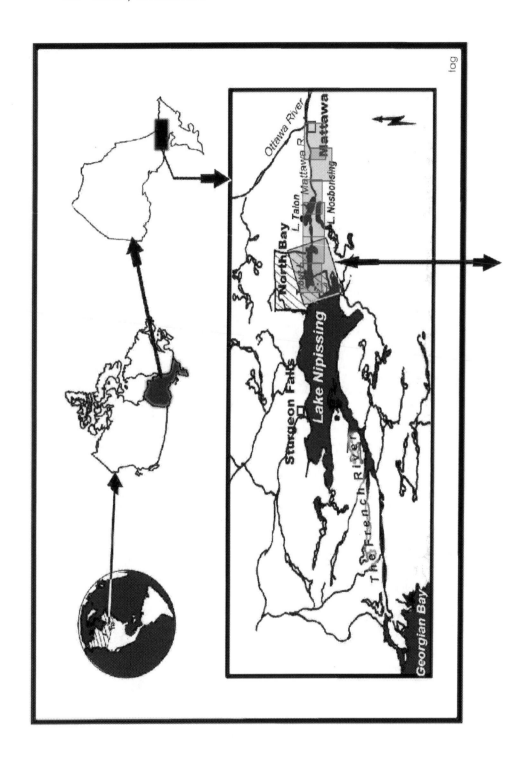

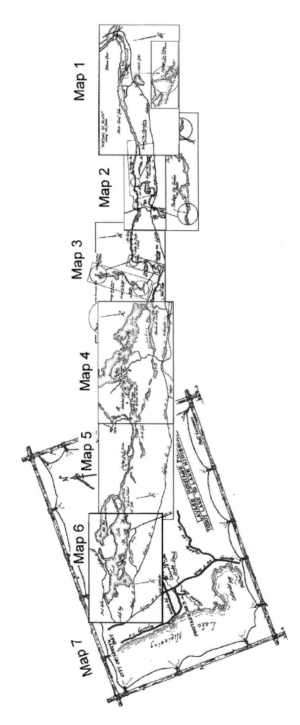

The illustration on the previous page demonstrates the location of the voyager canoe route being examined here relative to the Western Hemisphere. The above illustration demonstrates how the following maps are laid out east to west beginning from the Ottawa River onto the Mattawa River and ultimately to Lake Nipissing. The last map (Map 7) encompasses more area in order to detail the final and most complex part of the journey. This complexity is a result of the sudden change in the water table between Trout Lake and Lake Nipissing in that all waters from Trout Lake flow east to the Ottawa and all waters from Lake Nipissing flow west through the French River to the Great Lakes leaving no direct water route between the two.

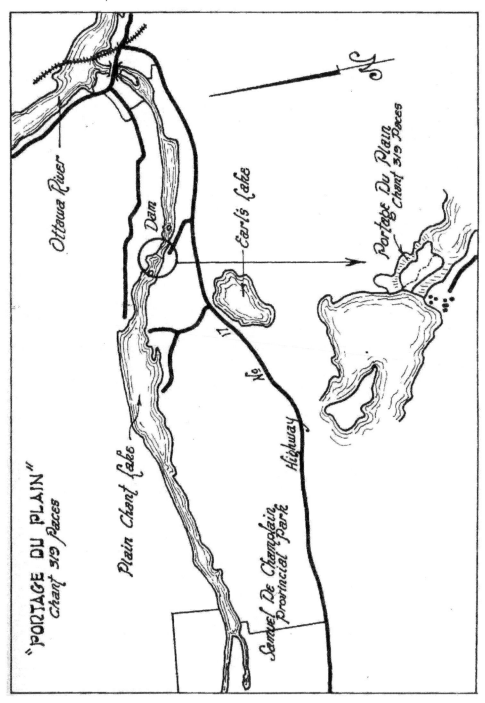

Map 1

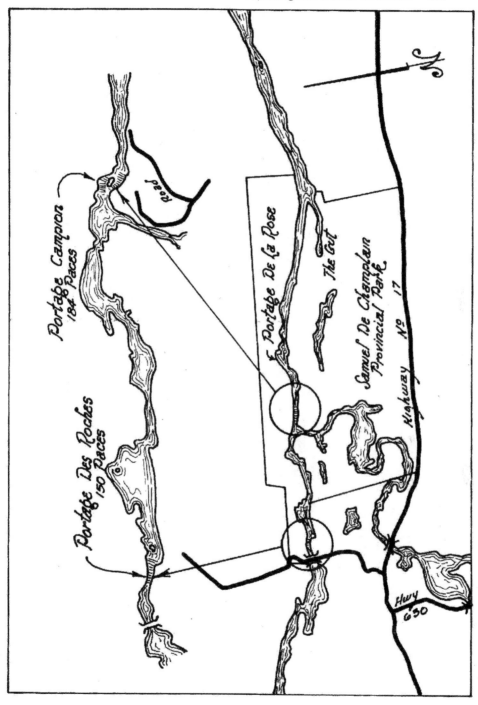

Map 2

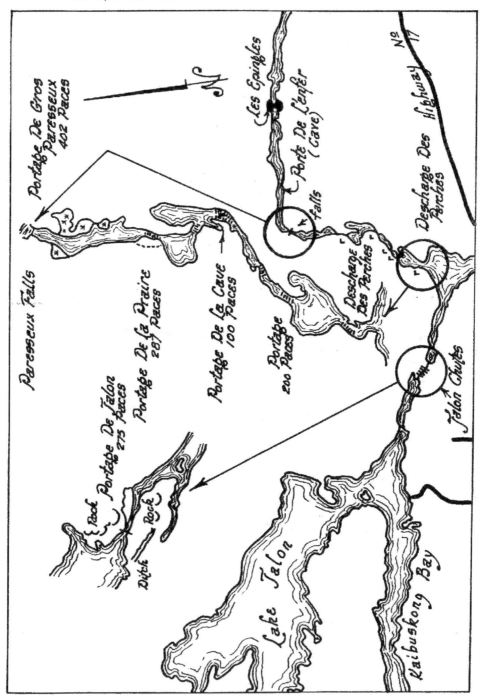

Map 3

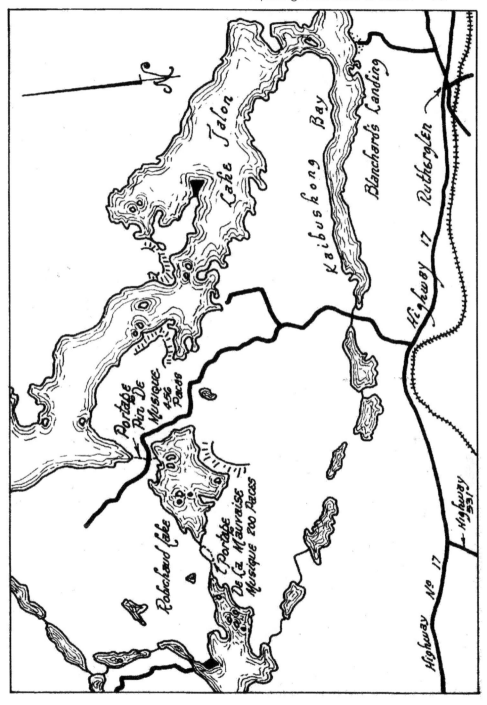

Map 4

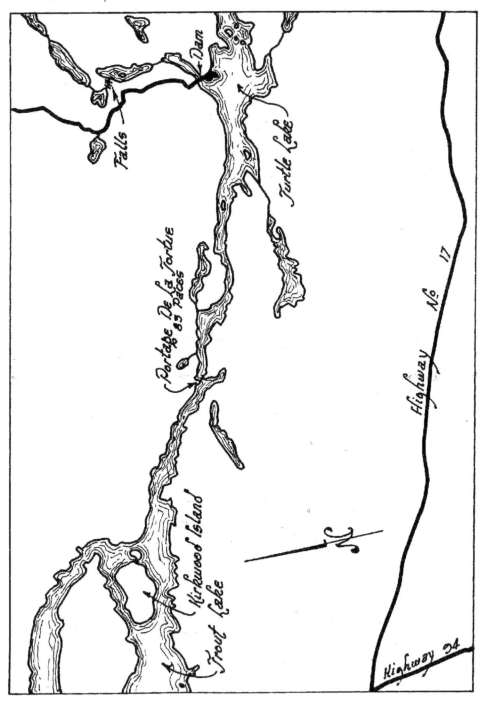

Map 5

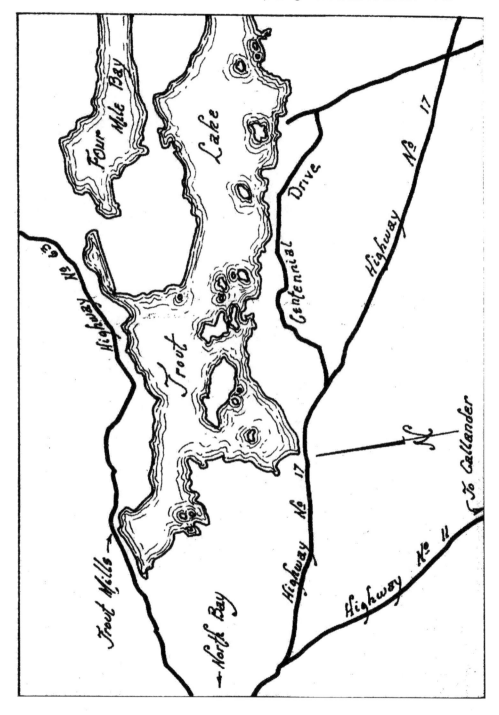

Map 6

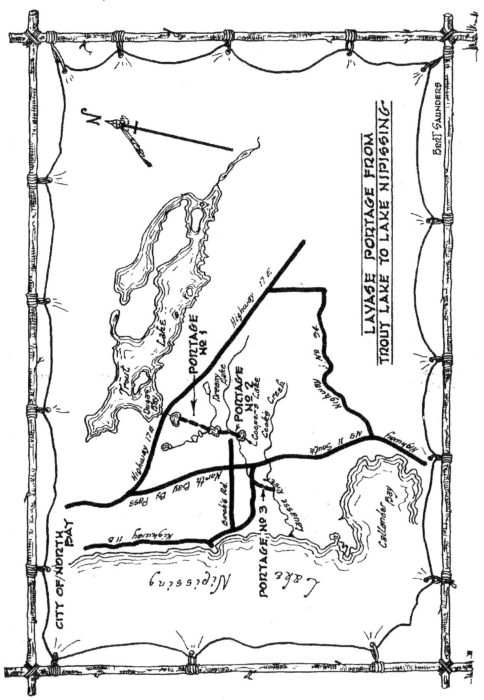

LAVASE PORTAGE FROM
TROUT LAKE TO LAKE NIPISSING

Map 7

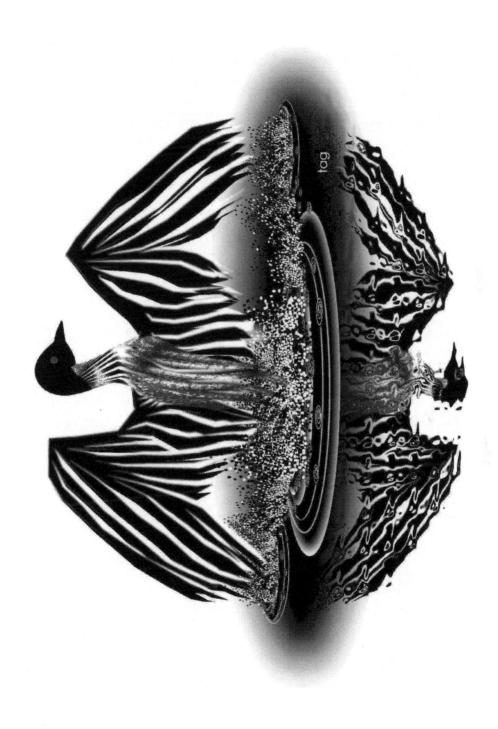

Chapter 9

The Hudson's Bay Company on Nipissing

In 1821 the Hudson's Bay Company absorbed the North West Company. Nicholas Garry, a deputy governor for the Hudson's Bay Company (1822-35), made a voyage of exploration over the old North West Company's territory. The following is taken from his diary re the Nipissing area.

Leaving the Utawa which at this Point is about 30 Leagues from the Timmiskamain Lake we enter the Petite Riviere or Mattawa and our Course which had hitherto been West and West-North-West is now South and South-West. The Mattawa is about 45 miles in length full of Rapids and Cataracts to its Source. After one Hour's paddling we came to the Portage de Pleins Champs, which is about 350 Paces. We then came to the Decharge of the Rose a hundred and fifty Paces. It now began to rain and our travelling was very uncomfortable being drenched with Rain and having no means to change our Linen and the Rain in wetting us whetted the Stings of our Enemies. We found at this Portage a Letter written on an Egg from Mr. McCloud, who had preceded us two Days, and the Smoking Bag belonging to Mr. Hughes which afterwards gave rise to a good Deal of Laughter [we] having pretended to have found a Billet d'Amour enclosed in the Bag.

We then passed the Decharge Campion, 120 Paces. We then came to the Portage of the Grosse Roche, 150 Paces. Here on a Piece of Bark was written a "Present to Mr. Garry" and on looking about we found a Pile of Stones and on removing them we found a small Land Tortoise which are very common in this Country. We then successively came to the Portage of Prairie, 287 Paces, then the Portage of La Cave, 100 Paces, then to the Portage of Talon, 300 Paces, the Country here is very wild and romantic. Going to the Top of a high Rock to view the surrounding Country I found a Sort of Flower Pot on a large and grand scale. The Water had excavated at the Top of the Rock a large round circular Hole exactly the Shape of a Flower Pot and in this a small beautiful Mountain Ash in full Verdure was growing. Here we dined at about 1/2 past 2. The Scenery about us was enchanting though it continued to rain at Intervals in Torrents. We dined on a high Rock beneath which was a Waterfall dashing over a rugged pointed Bed of Rocks and through a confined Passage, nearly 80 feet almost perpendicular Height. On this Portage the Trunk of a Tree is still to be seen which forms the Subject of the many numerous Stories of Disasters and Miseries with which this Journey abounds. During a stormy Day a Canoe passed under it at the Moment it fell. The Canoe and Men were dashed to Pieces and all were destroyed except one Man who had his leg broken and remained in this State for several Days without Assistance. During our Dinner a beautiful little Squirrel remained close to us seeming to enjoy our Company. We then embarked and came to the Portage de Pin de Musique which we did not find so terrific as described by MacKenzie. The Distance is about 450 Paces. The last Portage is the Turtle Portage when you come to the Lake of this Name where the Mattawa takes its source. On entering this Lake we met 4 Canoes with Indians with a Deputation of 80 Warriors going to Lord Dalhousie. One of the Indians had killed another and they were going to intercede for the Culprit. The Chief was a fine old Man apparently about 70, designated by the Feather in his flat, a common Goose Quill. The Young Men were very well looking. I only observed one Female who was probably the Wife of the Son of the Chief, as she was sitting behind him. She had a most beautiful intelligent Countenance the finest black Eyes and a Complexion that would have been considered as a Brunette and not darker in any Country. We made the Chief a Present of Tobacco and Biscuits. After passing this Lake we came to another, the passage from one to the other scarcely allowing space for our canoe. We then passed through a Succession of small Lakes and at 9 encamped on the last Vase. Our Journey has been this Day a most fatiguing one for our Men and the most miserable to us Bourgeois (so the Passengers who do not paddle are designated) comprehending almost everything, except meeting the beautiful Indian, which constitutes Misery in Travelling. We rose in the morning unrefreshed and exhausted by the Stings of our relentless Enemies who continued to pursue us during the Day. Soon after starting we were deluged with Rain and in this State were obliged to sit in our Canoe without the Opportunity of changing our Dress and attacked by the Mosquitoes and the little Sand Fly. In this State we arrived at our Encampment, the Name of the Vase or Morass gave us little Hope of Comfort and Rest. Scarcely had we landed when we were attacked by Myriads of Mosquitoes and Flies and Spiders; every Expedient was tried to drive them off but all without Effect and our Attempts only produced increased Irritation and Misery.

Wednesday the 20th (June). At 3 o'clock we started to walk 3 miles whilst our Canoe was towed thro' a small narrow Passage. We then embarked for a short Distance and landed at another Vase, the

Mosquitoes abounding in this swampy Ground. Here we had a short Walk when we found ourselves in a small beautiful Stream of Water about 40 yards broad and about 3 miles in Length. The Banks were beautiful, on one Side high grass and on the other the most beautiful forest trees. At once the Lake Nipissing came to our View and a Change from Misery to the greatest Pleasure and Comfort. Not the poor Wanderer in the Desert could be more delighted with the Sight of a Well after being parched with Thirst than we were on entering the Lake. Here we lost the Mosquitoes and bathing in the Lake restored us to Cleanliness and Comfort. At 9 we had breakfasted and started again. Lake Nipissingue is about 12 leagues in Length (though the Canoe course is more) and 15 miles broad. At 12, our Course W.S.W., we had made the grand Travers and came to a Point called the Isle aux Croix, so named from having 11 Crosses on it, the Tombs of 11 Voyageurs who were drowned. We now ran along the South Bank, low Land inky with the Pine Trees. There was a considerable Deal of Swell and it produced all the Feeling of Sea Sickness. At 1/2 past one we landed on a Rock to Dinner. Found a poisonous Plant which if touched produces Swelling to the Hand. At 1/2 past two embarked. Our course now is between Islands but barren Rocks and uninteresting.

The Hudson's Bay Company took over Fort Laronde, which, as has been noted in the previous chapter, had been moved to the north shore of Lake Nipissing. The name Fort Laronde fell into disuse and the fort was referred to simply as Nipissing Lake Post. In 1848 mention is made that the fort was moved to a new site, which I assume was on the right bank of the Sturgeon River near its mouth. It was on this site that a replica of the Post was built in 1967 as a centennial project of Springer Township, Cache Bay and the Historical Restoration Committee of the Sturgeon Falls Secondary School.

It seems strange that until the 1820's, the Nipissing Passage, so valuable to the fur trade, had only one post, Fort Laronde. Yet this ignored trading area met with strong rivalry during the 1800's. Fur traders from Newmarket and Penetang gave the Hudson's Bay Company fierce competition on Nipissing.

Today, North Bay boasts of being the Wild Fur Capital of the world under the management of Alex Shieff, of the Ontario Trappers Association. One trap line, entirely within the city limits of North Bay, worked by Jules Perron, produces annually a quota of beaver, comparable to any trap line in Canada. Indeed its harvest would have excited many of the early Hudson's Bay factors. In an age of fast depleting natural resources this says much for fur management.

The only other North West posts near us were Chats House and Fort Coulonge, both on the Ottawa River above the present city of Ottawa. The Hudson's Bay Company, however, expanded rapidly in the nineteenth century.

The Nipissing Post was part of a concentration of several others such as Mattawa House built in 1828, Fort Temiscaming (near Ville Marie) and five or six posts on and near Kipawa Lake. A few posts were built down the Ottawa, e.g. Dumoine as well as at Temagami, Matachewan, Whitefish Lake (near present Sudbury), and Cloche Island in the North Channel of Georgian Bay.

The following are excerpts from the Hudson's Bay diaries regarding the Nipissing post from 1821 until its closure in 1879. As far as I know there are no further diaries available, and I quote heavily from them since I feel they tell a fairly complete story of the Company on Nipissing.

It is interesting to note the first recorded murder on Nipissing involving whites. It appears that on December 15, 1844, a Company factor murdered one Etienne Rastool. Unfortunately the diary does not state whether Rastool was Indian or White. The literate of the day would spell a name as it sounded and undoubtedly "Rastool" meant "Restoule," a surname very familiar in the present Indian community. Reading through these and other diaries of the Company, one comes across several names (most often Scottish but also some French and English) that have been acquired by Indian families, although that is so in several cases. Often, however, Indians trading with a particular factor would name themselves or be named after the factor (e.g. McLeod's people or McKenzie's Indians). Thus for simplicity in a white man's world they acquired a white man's name. To add further confusion in tracing Indian genealogy, Christian names of fathers were often used as surnames by the sons. For example, the descendants of old Amable du Fond, may today be known as Mr. Amable or Mr. Dufond.

Thomas Cowburn and Toussaint de la Ronde were employed at Lake Nipissing by the united Hudson's Bay and North West Companies during the winter of 1821-22. On February 27, 1822, the Governor and Committee in London wrote to Governor William Williams of the Southern Department of the Company's territories:

With regard to the posts on the North Shore of Lake Huron and the Lake Nipissing, these also are exposed to opposition and will require great vigilance and activity in the management. It seems to be doubtful whether they can be more advantageously supplied by way of Michipicoten from Moose, or from Montreal, and this question ought to be minutely and carefully calculated and investigated, and that plan adopted which may appear upon the whole to be the best and most economical...

In 1823 it was decided that Lake Nipissing should be managed from Montreal by Thomas Thain, the Company's agent. Writing to him from London on March 29, 1823, the Company's Secretary remarked: "...The trade on Lake Huron and Lake Nipisingue must also be conducted on the Principle of gaining a very moderate profit or where opposed of only avoiding loss. But it is quite unnecessary to enter into a violent or extravagant competition, no private trader will continue opposition long, where he finds the above principle is steadily acted upon, and after a short time the field will be given up to the Company when moderate Profits may be made..."

During the winter of 1823-24 Toussaint La Ronde had charge of the Lake Nipissing post for the Hudson's Bay Company, but in the following winter Charles McKenzie looked after the Company's interests and La Ronde entered into opposition. On September 1, 1825, Chief Factor John McBean who was in charge of the Company's Lake Huron District, wrote to Messrs. McGillivrays, Thain and Company, its agents in Montreal:

Goods &cs. &cs. have been sent to Lake Nipisingue by the Drummond Island Traders (Rollette & Mitchell) and put in care of Mr. De La Ronde. The Robinsons, as well as Rae and Bollen of New Market it is said are to send each an Outfit there, I cannot say how far this is correct. However time will show. In short the oppositions are putting every Iron in the fire to enoy (sic) us, and to complete the whole have the vanity to say that they will drive us off of this part of the country...

McBean again wrote to the Montreal agents on March 5, 1826, informing them that the Newmarket interests of "Messrs. Robinson" and "Messrs Bollin & Rowe" had each established a post at the entrance of French River, and that he feared "if not soon stopped" they would soon reach Lake Nipissing. McBean mentioned that Mr. Donald McKay had traded for the Hudson's Bay Company at Lake Nipissing during 1825-26, and that "the opposition [La Ronde]" had not made much trade.

In the late summer and autumn of 1827 Francis Grant was in charge of the Hudson's Bay Company's trade on Nipissing, and on September 5, Governor George Simpson wrote to the Governor and Committee in London:

> *Lake Huron. This District comprehends seven Winter Establishments vizt. La cloche, Isle au Sables, Saguingue, Lake Nipisingue, White Fish Lake, Green Lake, Guard House and Grand Lac. The first situated on the Eastern bank of Lake Huron about halfway between the mouth of the French River and Sault Ste. Marys is the principal and only permanent post, the others being changed occasionally, in which we are influenced by the movements of the opposition and during the Summer abandoned, as no returns of any consequence could at that Season be collected and the people will then, in future be employed in the transport business of the District... Every part of this District is infested from time to time by opposition from Drummond Island, Sault Ste. Marys & New Market. The petty Traders are not people of weight or capital many of them being discharged Clerks & Interpreters of the late North West Coy. and of the American Fur Coy., who contrive to exist for a Season or two until their little means of credit are exhausted, but no sooner is one set put down than another appears, and being in the neighbourhood of Settlements, there is little prospects of the Honble. Coy. being left in the undisturbed possession of the Trade under any management or regulations. The point from which most danger is to be apprehended, is Lake Nipisingue from its proximity to Temiscamingue, but our attention is particularly directed to the protection of that quarter and I am in hopes that they have not sufficient weight to disturb the Trade of that valuable District. The only change of any importance that now remains to be effected in this quarter, is that of taking the returns to and outfitting the District from Moose Factory instead of Montreal, which will not only simplify and bring business under a more regular and uniform system of management but occasion a material reduction in the expenses. This will be commenced next Season and craft are now preparing for that purpose...*

In his report of the following year, 1828, dated July 10, Simpson remarked:

> *Lake Huron... There were last year seven Posts occupied by us in this District, at each of which, we were met by two oppositions so that in all there were Twenty one Trading Establishments in the*

District... The Principal opposition is from people of the name of Robertson at New Market, and their main object seems to be, to penetrate into Timiscamingue, but from the best information we have been unable to collect they are losing money and altho' they have now been three years established at Lake Nipisingue distant from Timiscaming Lake only 50 to 60 miles they have as yet made no impression in that quarter. We have a decided advantage over our opponents from the superior talent of our Traders, the quality of our Goods is moreover better, and our whole system of dealing is more regular, fair and liberal, so that when the Indians are left to themselves they always give us the preference, but they are constantly followed up during the winter by the petty Traders, who make liquor their principal article of barter, and such slaves are those unfortunate creatures to habits of intemperance that they cannot resist the temptation thus constantly held to their view, the consequence is that they are frequently cheated out of their hunt, by the petty Traders, and they in their turn cheat us out of the supplies that are advanced them on credit, as we cannot bring ourselves to, nor would Your Honors countenance us, in the iniquitous system of Trade pursued by our opponents. The District is this season attached to the Southern Factory and the necessary arrangements for the Transport of Outfits and returns between Moose and Michipicoten were all complete when I passed...

At the end of outfit 1828-29 Simpson wrote to the Governor and Committee in London:

Lake Huron. This District under the charge of Chief Factor McBain, was the only one in the Department which suffered materially by Opposition last year... The point in this District to which our attention is most particularly required is Lake Nipisang, on account of its proximity to Temiscamingue, there being only a neck of land of from 40 to 50 miles dividing the lakes of both names. Here we were for the three years previous to 1828 opposed by traders from New Market who made no impression, and gave up the contest after sustaining considerable loss, but they had not sooner disappeared that Day & McGillivray from the Ottawa river, (whom I have often had occasion to mention in my correspondence from Montreal) entered the lists. We are however prepared for them, and I am in hopes they will follow the example of those who preceded them. I do not see that any immediate change can be brought about in this District promising advantage to its interests, which receive that attention which their importance merits.

Messrs. Day & McGillivray "gave over the contests at Lake Nipisingue" about the spring of 1831 and it appears that shortly afterwards, Francis Grant, who was still trading for the Hudson's Bay Company, was opposed by Messrs. Harris & Peck.

The site of the Hudson's Bay Company's post on Lake Nipissing in 1830, like that of the North West Company's post of 1821, is in some doubt. The 1830 post was apparently somewhat off the direct route from Montreal to Fort William, for Governor Simpson's wife made no reference to it in the journal of her journey from Lachine to the Red River Settlement in that year. Mrs. Simpson gave a lengthy and lively description of a misadventure that happened to her travelling companion, Mrs. John George McTavish, on the "Prairie La Vase" Portage on May 10, and then continued:

> *After extricating her [Mrs. McTavish] with much difficulty, she was at length dragged to the end of the Portage, were we all washed and dried ourselves, and had breakfast, after which we descended a small river, passed thro' Lake Nipisang, about 40 miles in length, then made a Portage, into the French River...*

In his report on the trade of the Lake Huron District for the season of 1832-33, Chief Factor John McBean remarked:

> *...The fisheries throughout the District (except Green Lake and Nepisingue, where there is no fish) have been very good... The Gardens produced tolerably well, Lacloche had 547 Bushels potatoes..., at Nepisingue Mr. Grant had 60 Bushels potatoes. With this supply of fish and potatoes the Company's Servants have passed a good winter and afforded us the means of preventing the Indians from starving much... The Post of Lake Nepisingue has, by order of the Governor, been transferred to Temiscamingue District and has been given up at the close of Outfit 1832. This step I am afraid will not realise the benefit expected. At Lake Nepisingue the trade is very low, which is not the case at Lake Temiscamingue, where everything is more than 33 1/3 per cent dearer than at the former place. Will not this of itself cause much discontent among the Indians of Temiscamingue, when they find that those of Nepisingue get their wants much cheaper, and will it not be a sufficient cause for them to come privately and trade their furs with the opposition...*

During Outfit 1834-35 Charles Harris of the opposition firm of Harris and Peck entered the service of the Hudson's Bay Company. He was to have been in charge of the Company's post on Lake Nipissing, but when it was discovered that he would be opposed there by his "friend Peck", he was transferred to Timiskaming and Chief Trader Richard Hardisty took his place. At the end of season 1834-35 Samuel Peck, who had been trading on behalf of Andrew Mitchell of Penetanguishene, left the fur trade to take "an appointment of Captain in some Steamboat on Lake Huron."

Chief Trader Richard Hardisty continued to manage the Company's business on Lake Nipissing until the spring of 1837 when he was transferred to Kenogamissi District. He was succeeded on Nipissing by "Mr. Rodk. McKenzie late of Sturgeon Lake Albany District."

Reporting on the trade of Outfit 1836-37 to the Governor and Committee, Simpson remarked about the Timiskaming District:

> *This District is assailed by opposition from three different points, say Lake Nipisangue, Lac de Sable & the Ottawa River, and we are indebted for the protection in a great measure to the paucity of its natural resources in the means of subsistence there being no large animals in the District and very few fish in its waters, and to the attachment of the Indians to their Traders, who have great influence over them. The Lake Nipisangue opposition were very active during the past season but towards spring their provisions & goods became exhausted which operated against them...*

Roderick McKenzie continued in charge of the Hudson's Bay Company's post on Lake Nipissing. On December 15, 1844, he "deprived a fellow creature [Etienne Rastool] of life — apparently in self defence" and early in January 1845 Charles de la Ronde arrived from Penetanguishene to arrest him. McKenzie left Francois Fortier in temporary charge of the Company's business. McKenzie, it appears, was tried for murder, but was acquitted. He returned to his duties at Lake Nipissing, but on September 10, 1845, Sir George Simpson informed the Governor and Committee in London:

> *...The post of Lake Nipissingue has been very much mismanaged of late by the Clerk in charge, Roderick McKenzie... This unfortunate man, it was discovered, had fallen into intemperate habits, which led to the business under his charge being very much neglected, & the post being off the line of communication, it was inconvenient to visit it, so, that, his mismanagement & bad habits went for a length of time before they were discovered... he was... removed at a moment's notice this Autumn, and [John] McLeod, and Apprentice Clerk of last year,*

sent from Lake Huron to relieve him...

McLeod left Lake Nipissing post at the end of Outfit 1845-46 and for a short time the trade was in the care of Goulet, senior.

The next Hudson's Bay company employee to be in charge at Lake Nipissing was Sir George Simpson's brother-in-law and cousin, John Wedderburn Simpson. He went there in the summer of 1846. In autumn, 1847, James Cameron, then in charge of the Timiskaming District, requested "that a young horse for Lake Nipisingue... should be forwarded from Fort Coulonge." This request was held up by Sir George Simpson until he could "learn the particular object" for which the horse was intended. Cameron replied from Timiskaming on January 31, 1848:

> *...With regard to the Horse requested for Nepisingue — the[y] have had one there since '38. It was essentially necessary on account of the distance of the Establishment from Firewood being fully three miles — but as the buildings are to be removed in the Spring to a proper place — one will not be so necessary than for that purpose — but I think a Horse would be very useful for Farming purposes, with such a soil and climate as they have there, they ought to raise produce for a part of the expenditure at least — there is little or no danger in sending up one from Mattawa after the Transport is over — the Lumberers having clear paths the worst part of the way. There never were Horses reared at this place — the first Horses brought here was when the Lumber business commenced and they are both old now....*

Governor Simpson sanctioned a horse being sent to Lake Nipissing and it appears that during the summer of 1848 a start was made on the buildings for the new site mentioned in the above extract. This work, however, had to be held up until a carpenter could be sent from Albany Factory, the men at Lake Nipissing being an "awkward set". No further information concerning this move has so far been found in our archives, but we notice that at the time of the publication of Dr. Bigsby's The Shoe and Canoe in 1850 he recorded that "La Ronde" post was "now removed to an island on the north shore, halfway between the Vaz River and River des Francois," and continued, saying, "It is considered to be eight or ten miles out of the canoe route to St. Mary's from Montreal."

During the summer and autumn of 1854 Mr. Alexander Murray of the Geological Survey of Canada wrote that he was engaged in making exploratory surveys to the east of Lake Huron and Georgian Bay.

These included a survey of the southern shore of Lake Nipissing, from the point where the French River measurement ceased in 1847, to the mouth of the Vase, where connection was made with Sir William Logan's survey of 1845, and thence of the north shore of this sheet of water to its "north-west angle".

In 1855, Mr. Murray continued this survey, commencing at the outlet of Lake Nipissing into the French River, along the western coast making connection with the work of the previous year. In 1856 this survey was again extended, this time a start being made from the Hudson's Bay Company's Post on Sturgeon River near Lake Nipissing.

John Wedderburn Simpson remained in charge at Lake Nipissing from 1846 until he was transferred to Timiskaming for Outfit 1850-51. He appears to have been succeeded at Nipissing by John Cormack, an interpreter, and on January 5, 1852, J.W. Simpson wrote to the Governor Simpson from Timiskaming:

> There is a demand for Cranberries in Lake Huron. Near the post at Lake Nipissing is a meadow or Swamp in which they grow abundantly, and I have to beg you will make arrangements for collecting as large a quantity as possible, employing your men in gathering and also Indians, to be paid at so much a bushel for what they deliver, you can pack them in barrels and bags and send them down to Lacloche this fall, say in September or October at the least, the sooner the better. It is probable a Surveyor [Walter Shanly, acting under instructions from the commissioner of Public Works] may be sent to Nepisingue this fall to make a plan of the location. You, for the Company, should include the Cranberry meadow if possible....

It will be noticed that the extract from the report of the Geological Survey mentions "the Hudson's Bay Company's Post on Sturgeon River near Lake Nipissing". This was the post J.S. Ironside was in charge of, for we have found two letters from him dated December 5, 1856, one written from "Sturgeon River, Lake Nipisingue" and the other from "Sturgeon Hall, Lake Nipissing."

On September 27, 1857, John W. Simpson wrote to Sir George Simpson from Timiskaming: "...Opposition is expected up from Lake Huron at Nepisingue, the Cranberry meadow are perfectly overflown & no fruit to be procured...."

On September 27 of the following year R.S. Miles wrote to Sir George from La Cloche: "...Mr. Crawford on his way down the French River met another Trader going to establish at Nipisingue. His name is

John Murray from Killarden and has two Canoes laden with goods & provisions. Mr. Ironside is therefore likely to be as strongly opposed as our Friends of Temiscaming Lake...."

On November 12, 1862, Chief Factor Edward M. Hopkins wrote from Montreal to Peter W. Bell at La Cloche:

...With reference to the Nipisingue post, I have frequently heard that the system under which the trade is there conducted is unsuited to the present times & state of the country. It appears we adhere to the old-fashioned tariffs & system of trade that our officers do not run about in search of furs or to watch the opposition, in short that we sleep our post & allow our petty rivals to creep into the country & run off with the bulk of the furs. The Agents of Thompson of Penitanguishene, make at Nipisingue their principal collections. Mr. R. Crawford, who is at present here, confirms these rumours.

It is absolutely necessary to put a check to this state of affairs, even in the absence of the Governor (Dallas) & without the previous sanction of Council. I, therefore, assume the responsibility of placing the post of Nipisingue under your supervision for the coming winter, feeling assured my act will hereafter be sustained. It will still remain an outpost of Temiscamingue.... Mr. Ironside is instructed to look to you for order & to adopt such changes in the system of trade as may appear to be more immediately necessary....

As soon as you can spare the time, you should take a run to Nipissing to consult with Mr. Ironside & to make your arrangements for co-operation, chiefly with a view to check the encroachments of free traders in that direction, more especially Ducas & others in the employ of Mr. Thompson of Penitanguishene....

J.W. Simpson protested at the removal of the Nipissing Lake post from his charge, but Hopkins stood by his instructions and wrote to Bell on April 1, 1863:

What I desire you to do, is to infuse new life and activity into the management, & to adopt such changes in the system of trade there, as may secure the returns for the Company, instead of allowing them to fall so largely as they have lately done into the hands of Thompson's people....

William H. Watt succeeded J.S. Ironside at Nipissing in the summer of 1863 and the post was transferred to the Lake Huron District. In 1864 Watt was succeeded by Edward Sayer and the correspondence of the time continues to refer to the strong opposition in the area from "Mr. Thompson's Trader [Ducas, or 'Dokis']". Sayer left the Company at the close of Outfit 1865-66 and his place at Nipissing was taken up by Walter Colvile.

Roderick McKenzie wrote to Edward M. Hopkins from La Cloche on August 6, 1866:

> *I found the Post of Nepissingue in rather a forlorn state. The appearance is sufficient to show that the people in charge of the place for the last few years did not display much of their energy or industry. Tis true the dwelling house is pretty good but it is over a quarter of a mile from the store & men's house as well as the stables all of these buildings are in a dilapidated state the Store threatening to fall in the river & the men's house sinking with rottenness but I need not waste your time in describing it as you must have seen it in passing in that direction so often. I may remark that it is rather a disgrace to the Coy. to have their establishment in such state when a poor Indian in the neighbourhood (Duckers) is rearing up a two-story house &c. painted, shingled & plastered I actually saw Casks of lime & coal oil on the portages for that purpose ["Duckers" refers to Michael Dokis]. He is displaying great activity this summer. While I was at Nepissingue canoes were expected to leave with provisions &c. for Metaugum & Abitibi and other places. I left Cummings up there but don't expect much from his activity or usefulness. He complained once for being watched and hard pressed since I came here would only perform a certain amount of work and anything new was quite against his grain....*

Walter Colvile, who arrived at the Nipissing post early in October, 1866, was assisted by Norman McLeod and they found the opposition traders very active. During the winters of 1867-68 and 1868-69 Charles Crawford had charge of the post and Norman McLeod continued as assistant. McLeod was considered the better man but "his want of education" was an obstacle to his having charge of the post. However, in 1869, this "most honest person" who, "from his long residence & connection by marriage to the Indians" was a useful man to the Company, was put in charge of the Nipissing post and was given a young assistant to keep the accounts. On June 24, 1871, Chief Trader Roderick McKenzie wrote from La Cloche to James Bissett at Montreal saying that "...The Post of Nipissing has improved... under the management of Norman McLeod an old Servant who has now been many years at the place", and in a report on the Nipissing post dated May 7, 1872, McKenzie junior, a son of the Chief Trader, remarked:

Fur-bearing animals are obviously scarce in this part of the country, especially Beaver — being almost extinct in the lands bordering on the Lake which is chiefly owing to the depredation of the Indians on one another's land. Red deer are considerably plentiful on the southern side of the lake, and Moose have lately begun to appear in the immediate vicinity of the post…. With regard to the future before this post, the increase of petty traders and the apparent scarcity of fur-bearing animals, render it difficult to determine what it may be. In a general view, the prospects are by no means promising. We can furnish no particular plan that could be adopted to improve or preserve the Trade: the conducting of the business must necessarily depend on the movements of the Opposition….

During the winter of 1872-73 McLeod, who could neither read nor write, was at the Nipissing post alone owing to the difficulty in getting a clerk to assist him, but during Outfit 1873-73 T.E. Wilson kept the accounts and did the clerical work for him. On July 28, 1876, Factor Joseph Hardisty wrote from La Cloche to James Bissett in Montreal:

…Nipissing again shows a heavy loss, and it will be for you or the Chief Commissioners to say whether or not we should restrict our operations in that quarter. That Nipissing is not of late years showing any Profit is not that McLeod is wanting in his duty. He is on the contrary most diligent and attentive, but he has great odds to contend against. His circuit is overrun with opposition Traders & the Furs he does get he has necessarily to pay very high prices for. There is little doubt at the same time that the check McLeod gives the opposition around Nipissing very materially helps Temiscaming & other stations further inland, & while we in this District derive no advantage from our operations there, the Company, as a whole, do or do at more remote stations inland, and taking into consideration this view of the case I have again outfitted Nipissing pretty largely to Outfit 1876….

In the summer of 1876 George Goldsworthy, apprentice Clerk, was sent to Nipissing to replace E.T. Wilson as assistant, and during most of the winter of 1877-78, when Norman McLeod was ill, Goldsworthy had to manage the business. This was at a time when the opposition in the Lake Huron District was very strong, "Thompson of Penitanguishene" having "four traders up in the Nipissing quarter".

On December 13, 1878, George McKenzie in charge of the Lake Huron District wrote from La Cloche to Bissett mentioning the "Railway now building in the vicinity of Lake Nipissing" and adding,

...As Nipissing post has not paid for some time back and as there is no great prospect of its ever paying again, I would advise that it be closed at the close of this Outfit (1878-79), and a post opened in its stead at Lake Wanapitaping....

Nipissing Lake Post was closed in the summer of 1879 and the stock of goods on hand removed to Wanapitaping. Norman McLeod, who was still a sick man, remained in charge of the lands and buildings for the Company until his death in the summer of 1880.

In 1882 the Hudson's Bay Company applied to the Ontario Government for a grant of land at the Lake Nipissing post, which was still closed, and by 1885, 288 acres, being Lot No. 8 in Concession B, Township of Springer, District of Nipissing, were registered in its name. This position is clearly marked on the right bank of Sturgeon River on Map 606 accompanying Vol. X (1897) of the Geological Survey of Canada. This map is entitled "Nipissing District, Ontario and Pontiac Co., Quebec."

tag

John Rudolphus Booth
*In thirty years he went from carpenter to lumber king, with lumber,
pulp and paper mills on the Ottawa River, and vast timber holdings
across Northern Ontario.*

Chapter 10

The Arrival of the Lumberman

Although the story of the lumbermen will be told in full in a future publication, their activities do dovetail with the story of the fur trade and thus warrant some mention here.

As early as 1848 Colin Rankin of Mattawa House makes mention in his diary of various activities of the shanty men along the Ottawa and Mattawa Rivers. In the Autumn of 1847 James Cameron, head of the Temiskaming district, requested a horse be delivered from Fort Coulonge on the Ottawa River to the Nipissing post. He says, "There is little or no danger in sending up one from Mattawa — the Lumberers having clear paths the worst part of the way." Apparently logging operations had reached the shore of Lake Nipissing in a haphazard method as early as 1847. These were probably the roads and paths that brought the first livestock of the pioneers to the south shore of Lake Nipissing before the building of the Nipissing road from Rousseau in 1874-75.

These early loggers were made up of individual families and maybe a few employees who simply cut the easily available timber along the riverbanks, and floated it downstream to the markets at Bytown (Ottawa) or Montreal. The first truly organized lumber company to enter Nipissing was the J.R. Booth Company.

John Rudolphus Booth, carpenter, and his young wife, Roselinda, moved from Quebec's eastern townships to Bytown in 1852. In time he set up a small lumber mill, lost it by fire, and built again. He won, by audacious bids, large timber rights at auction and supplied white pine for the Canadian Parliament building then being erected. Within thirty years he was lumber king of the Ottawa Valley, with lumber, pulp and paper mills on the Ottawa, and vast timber holdings across northern Ontario.

Booth probably started logging the Amable du Fond River and Lake Nosbonsing area in the late 1860's, arriving at the Depot Creek operations (Chisholm Township) in 1870. These operations created no problems to Booth as the logs were cut, hauled and dumped into the tributaries of the Mattawa River, from which there was easy access to the Ottawa mills.

When his jobbers started cutting along the Wasi Creek, a geographical problem arose. The Wasi drains into Lake Nipissing thus over the height of land, and away from the Ottawa watershed. The company planned to build a dam at the outlet, where the Wasi Creek enters Wistawasing Lake, to allow this water to flood into Depot Creek thus affording them a direct route to the Mattawa. The government refused them permission to do this. It was then necessary to build a dam at the outlet of Wasi Lake, to create a reserve of water to float logs on down the river to Lake Nipissing. By this route Booth missed the natural drainage to his mill, and therefore the company had to devise a method of returning the logs to the desired location.

A railroad was built from the top of the Wasi escarpment to Lake Nosbonsing. The waterpower of the Wasi Falls was utilized to operate an elaborate jack-ladder (a type of endless chain operating inside a wooden frame to move logs from a lower to a higher area, often used to lift logs from a holding pond into the saw mill). From here they were loaded onto flat cars, taken across the tracks and dumped into Nosbonsing.

This operation started shortly after the arrival of the C.P.R. on the shores of Nipissing, probably around 1883. The engine used on these tracks was brought into the area via the C.P.R., was eased down the embankment onto a barge (near the present site of the government wharf at North Bay), towed to Callander Bay, and was eased up the escarpment at Wasi Falls to the waiting tracks. The flat cars used in this creation were likewise moved to the site. After setting up this operation the Booth Lumber Co. had access to Lake Nipissing and its tributaries. This entire operation was placed under the supervision of Thos. Darling. The remains of the Booth track today is a paved road leading from Highway 11 to Astorville.

tag

INDEX

Illustrations

Selected Readings

Bishop, Morris. Champlain—The Life of Fortitude. Toronto: McClelland and Stewart, 1963.

Copway, C. The Traditional History and Characteristic Sketches of the Ojibway Nation. Toronto: Coles Publishing, 1973.

Cranston, J.H. Étienne Brulé—Immortal Scoundrel. Toronto: Ryerson Press, 1949.

Edmunds, Walter. The Musket and the Cross. New York: Little, Brown, 1968.

Grier, Rev. J. Sylvester. The History of St. Ann's Parish. Sudbury: Comité des fêtes du cinquantenaire de la Paroisse Sainte-Anne, 1933.

Hallaran, Joan. The History of the Mattawa Wild River Park. Ministry of Natural Resources.

Henry, Alexander. Travels and Adventures In Canada and the Indian Territories between the Years 1760-1776. Edmonton: M.G. Hurtig, 1969.

Lamb, W. Kaye (ed.). The Journals and Letters of Sir Alexander MacKenzie. Cambridge: Cambridge University Press, 1968.

Martineau Donat. Le Fort Timiskaming. [2e éd.] Rouyn, Québec: Société Saint-Jean-Baptiste de l'ouest québécois, 1970.

Nute, Grace Lee. The Voyageur. Minneapolis: Minnesota Historical Society, 1954.

Sagard, Rev. Gabriel. The Long Journey to the Country of the Hurons. Trans. H.H. Langton. Toronto: Champlain Society, 1939.

Surtees, Robert. The Original People. Toronto: Holt Rinehart and Winston, 1971

Tooker, Elizabeth. An Ethnography of the Huron Indians. 1615-1649. Smithsonian Institution Bureau of Ethnology Bulletin 190. 1964.

Thwaite, (ed.) Jesuit Relations and Allied Documents. Boston: Burrows Brothers, 1898.

About the Cover:

("The Nipissing Tree" by T. A. Grainger)

Stained in the pigment of the Holy and the Sovereign
reality is transformed
a reflection of the spiritual and cultural changes
forever altering the land and its occupants

Rising from the forest
Michabo
the great spirit of the Algonquin
revealed within the power and dignity of the eagle
continues to nurture and protect
offering sanctuary for those seeking renewal

The good spirit Manitou
manifest within the Nipissing Tree
the tangible connection between man and nature
reaches into the past
to maintain its spiritual sustenance

Sheltered by the sanctum of the Michabo
and nurtured through its roots to the past
the Nipissing Tree remains untouched by the stain of change

Their gazes subdued
both spiritual representations ponder an uncertain future
for all they represent

Lost within the consequence of change
the Children of the Nipissing
no longer play within the branches of the Nipissing Tree
but remain scattered among the greater Algonquin Nation